Born into the
Poor Law

*The children
of Barnstaple Workhouse
& Cottage Homes*

Gudrun Limbrick

First published in 2025 by Memories in Print
Ilfracombe, North Devon

ISBN 978-0-9931432-8-1

Printed and bound in the UK by 4Edge, Hockley.

This book is dedicated to all those
who spent in time in
Barnstaple's Workhouse
or the Cottage Homes

About the author

For nearly twenty years, Gudrun has been working to share information about former children's homes in the UK and the lives of children taken into residential institutions. During the course of her work as a social researcher, she interviewed hundreds of people who had spent some or all of their childhoods in children's homes. It became clear from this that there was a need for accessible information about people's own childhoods and the children's homes they were in.

Determined to do something about this she set up a website in 2011 dedicated to sharing information, photos and memories about children's homes. Selling books about memories of the homes raises funds to keep the website going.

Now living in Ilfracombe, Gudrun studied at and attained degrees from the University of Oxford and the University of Birmingham.

Former Children's Homes
www.formerchildrenshomes.org.uk

sharing memories and information
about former children's homes, orphanages,
cottage homes and other institutions for children

Contents

Introduction

When Oliver Twist asked for more, he was representing one of many children living in English workhouses. The nineteenth century was a time of enormous change, change which brought great wealth to some and poverty to thousands of others. People were left unemployed by industrialisation and the mechanisation of farm work, and displaced by urbanisation. There was no NHS to help people when they were ill; no benefits to help people when they could not afford to feed their families and few places to seek shelter when a family had no home.

Workhouses, established by the Poor Laws, were lauded as cheap places to house the poor but were also intended to be a deterrent to others thinking of putting themselves at the mercy of the workhouse.

This book tells the story of the children of the workhouse in Barnstaple and follows them as they moved into the Cottage Homes. The story is told using only sources of information written at the time of the events described.

Full names have not been used, and some identifying characteristics have been removed, to respect the privacy of the families concerned. However, the stories are all based on the truth as it was told and understood at the time.

During the course of the decades since the workhouses dominated social care in England, language has evolved significantly keeping pace with our growth in understanding of people and the world around us. This is certainly true of the language we use to describe disabilities, mental illness, illegitimacy and women. What were once primitive medical terms or formal speech have now become derogatory and offensive.

Where I have quoted original text, some of these terms have been incorporated. No offence is intended, but I use them to reflect the perceptions of mental illness, disabilities and illegitimacy at that time.

I tell the stories of children who were in workhouses, cottage homes and other institutions because they are stories which are otherwise destined to be forgotten like, so often, the people themselves. They are however, a significant part of our history and thus a fundamental part of our present and future.

Gudrun Jane Limbrick, May 2025

Barnstaple's Workhouse

In the early nineteenth century, poverty in Britain was rife. There was high unemployment and many of the jobs that did exist were low-paid or insecure. There was a new mobility with people leaving their home parishes to travel to towns and cities generally in search for work.

Support for people in need was through the Poor Laws which had put the parish church at the centre of care for those in need since 1601. Local ratepayers gave money which was handed out to the poor by the church. Some areas also had their own poorhouses or workhouses such as Ilfracombe (Church Steps) and Combe Martin (Church Street). Barnstaple (Tuly Street). However, by the early 1800s, it was thought that this small scale approach was no longer effective.

The solution, it was decided, was to group parishes together into Poor Law Unions which could build and run much larger workhouses. The idea was enshrined in the Poor Law Act of 1834 and there followed a period of huge investment in new workhouse buildings throughout the country.

The Barnstaple Borough Poor Law Union, comprising all the surrounding parishes, began work to establish a new Union workhouse to replace all the small parish poorhouses. The first step was to find somewhere to put it.

Ground for a Workhouse

WANTED, A PIECE OF GROUND, situate
not exceeding Four Acres in extent, for
the site of a Workhouse
for the Barnstaple Union.

Proposals of terms to be sent to the Clerk to the
Board of Guardians on or before
the 22nd day of January 1836

The site chosen was east of Barnstaple, away from the quay, streets and houses. Behind the workhouse was Fort Hill. At that time, the town had around 7,000 inhabitants, a figure 2,000 higher than nearby Bideford, and making the town around a fifth the size of Exeter. Barnstaple was known for its annual fair each September. The first few days of the fair were primarily focused on buying and selling livestock and the last day, falling on a Friday, was devoted to fun and entertainment. People flocked there from all around to buy, sell and enjoy themselves. The new workhouse would mean that people from the region now had another reason to come into Barnstaple, but the institution was certainly not about fun and entertainment.

Sampson Kempthorne, who designed other workhouses in Devon including those at Crediton and South Molton, was chosen as the architect of the new workhouse. Barnstaple's Guardians of the Poor, nervous of the expense, asked him to modify his usual cruciform design so that it could accommodate 200 people rather than 300 but with scope for an extension to be built in the future should it be needed. Inmates of the old Barnstaple parish workhouse on Tuly Street were put to work on completing the new workhouse although a number were sentenced to time in Exeter Gaol when they refused to do the work.

In 1837, when the workhouse build was nearing completion, the Guardians posted an advert for a Master and Matron to run it, the key attribute sought being that the couple 'must be able to keep accounts'.

Wanted by the Board of Guardians
for this Union

A Master and Matron of the New Union Workhouse
at Barnstaple. They must be able to keep accounts,
produce satisfactory testimonials of character and
efficiency, and give security to the amount of £100
for the faithful discharge of their duties.

Closing all the local parish poorhouses and having just one large workhouse in their place was a huge investment but was intended, in the longer term, to reduce costs significantly. Staff numbers would be reduced, with the single large workhouse being run by a master and a matron, a porter, a nurse, a cook and some general servants as the basic staff team. Food and other items were bought in large quantities by the cheapest local suppliers.

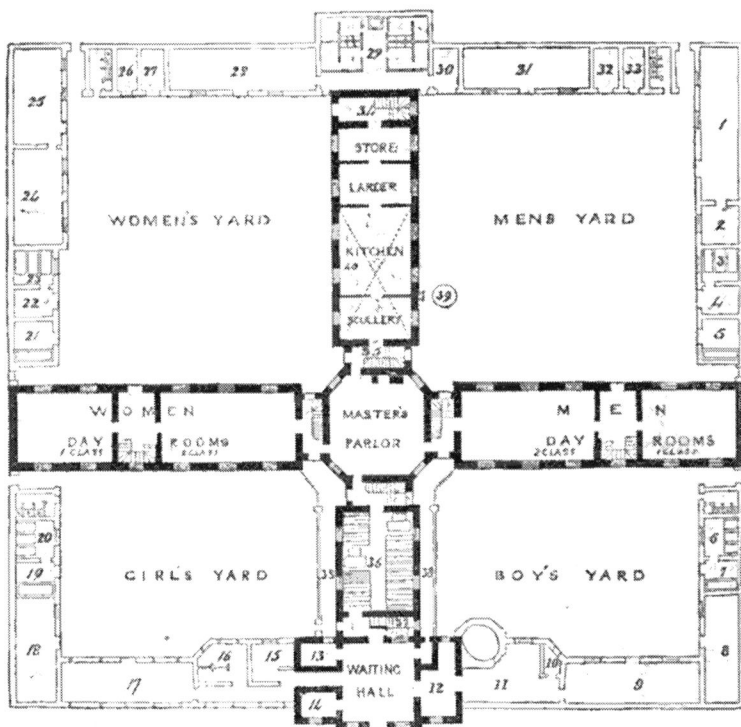

A cruciform workhouse plan by Sampson Kempthorne who was the architect of Barnstaple workhouse and a number of other English workhouses

The new Barnstaple Poor Law Union Workhouse was managed by a board of local people known as the Guardians of the Poor. They had the power to assess each individual's level of need and grant cash payments to keep them going (known as outdoor relief or outrelief) or, if there were no other options, a stay in the workhouse (indoor relief). Each Guardian was elected to represent one of the parishes that comprised the Union. Barnstaple Poor Law Union was made up of 40 parishes[1] in the area within Lynton to the north, Mortehoe to the west, Atherington to the south and Challacombe to the east.

With between one and four people representing each parish (depending on the size of the parish), the Barnstaple Guardians of the Poor numbered around 120 of whom perhaps 20 would attend each fortnightly meeting. To stand for election as a Guardian, a person had to be a property owner paying rates of more than £15 a year, a high level. And, until 1875, they had to be a man. It was not until the 1890s that women were elected to the Barnstaple Board.

The Guardians elected from their number a chair, and they had a paid clerk who arranged the meetings and carried out all the administration and correspondence. The Master of the workhouse provided each meeting with records of all outgoings and notes of all the issues needing the Guardians' consideration. From 1871, Poor Law Unions were overseen by the Local Government Board, a British Government department.

Workhouses were meant to be a last resort. They were an expensive investment and so only those in dire straits would be admitted. To keep costs down, home comforts were few and far between and the diet meagre. In return, the inmate was given monotonous, hard work to do. If a person caused trouble, refused to

---

BARNSTAPLE UNION

T HE Board of Guardians are desirous of being supplied with a plain light one-horse HEARSE on four wheels, for the conveyance of such poor persons who die in the Union Workhouse to their own parishes for internment. Sealed applications with a drawing of the proposed vehicle, and the price intended to be charged for the same, must be sent to JS CLAY, Clerk.
Barnstaple July 11th 1836

10

work, or escaped, fines or prison sentences were handed out.

Nothing about a person's stay in the workhouse was to be sufficiently pleasant to encourage them to stay for any longer than was absolutely necessary. Laziness was forbidden and punishments were severe. Because of the harshness of the workhouse, or The House, as it was known locally, it was a feared place in the town.

The workhouse had all the harshness, discipline and structure of a prison although the people were not in there because they had committed a crime. There was a general perception that unemployment was due to the laziness of the individual rather than a shortage of work. The workhouse was intended to put a stop to this.

While there certainly were many who went into the workhouse because they were destitute through unemployment, many went there because they could not physically work including those who were elderly and infirm. Women who were about to give birth and could not afford medical care or had no one to look after them would go to the workhouse for weeks or months. While any woman could end up having to have her child in the workhouse, it was particularly common for those who were not married to give birth in the House People with disabilities or mental illness might also find themselves in the workhouse if they could not work and there was nowhere else appropriate for them to live. There were institutions for people with particular conditions such as the Starcross Idiot Asylum which was established in the nineteenth century in Teignmouth. The term 'idiot' was originally a medical term used to describe people with learning disabilities. However, such places were few and far between in Devon and places were limited. Often the workhouse was the only option.

There were also much stranger reasons for going into the workhouse:

————❖————

Ann's story

A married man, it was alleged in court in 1836, was in the habit of meeting Ann, described as a young girl of 'weak intellect'. He would insist she went with him to a pub on Bear Street. Ann said he made her drink beer by threatening to throw it in her face if she refused. When Ann's mother remonstrated with him about this, he threatened that he would do worse to Ann if her mother didn't leave him alone. The matter came to court because, on her way home from one of these sessions in the pub, Ann was attacked and pushed to the ground by three boys, and rescued by a neighbour. The magistrate said he could not find the boys guilty because the only witness, the neighbour, had not seen the attack itself, only the boys standing around Ann on the ground and that Ann herself was not capable of giving her side of the story. Of the man who enticed her into the pub he said "he could not speak but in terms of the greatest indignation". The magistrate said that "the unfortunate girl should be removed into the workhouse where she might be protected from the rudeness and insults of designing men and wanton boys".

This Poor Box was placed on the wall of the Guildhall in 1895 hoping to attract donations to help the Borough look after its poor population. The initials SB are for Samuel Berry who was Mayor of Barnstaple in 1894 and 1895. Recently refurbished, the box is still in place.

As was the case with so many Union workhouses, it was sited in the countryside on the edge of the urban area, but was soon surrounded by housing as the town grew. Initially, the building had gardens which were tended by the inmates to grow vegetables to add to the diet of the inmates and officers. Much of that land was then sold off and Alexandra Road, initially a track for horses and carts, came to split the original workhouse land in two.

The workhouse had coal heating and was lit by oil lamps. The residents slept in dormitories, with a dayroom or workroom. Men were separated from women, an children separated from the adults, splitting families up. The daily regime was structured and rigid to ensure the residents were manageable. Small courtyards enabled inmates to have some fresh air.

Residents, or inmates as they were known, were woken at daybreak, they washed in cold water, ate a meagre cold breakfast, and worked until the next meal time. It was a basic and plain diet of food such bread, meat, potatoes and oats. A chapel on site meant that the inmates could worship. Visitors were not invited. Despite the large numbers of people living there, it could be a lonely existence.

BARUM WORKHOUSE
1887: Starling Pie

A meeting of the Board of Guardians heard complaints had been received about shooting starlings on Fort Hill causing annoyance to women who liked to walk there. They said they were being peppered with falling shot. The starlings were to be made into pies, starling pie being a favourite of the Master of the workhouse. "Everyone will agree with Mr Langdon that, if the Governor of the Barnstaple Union Workhouse likes starling pie there is no reason why he should not have it. But if it be necessary to the obtaining of the admitted luxury that ladies walking over Fort Hill shall be peppered with falling shot, the moral law which limits liberty when it takes upon itself the form of license steps in." The Guardians agreed that the shooting of the hapless birds was to take place elsewhere and leave the women in peace. "The peppering, if peppering there must be, should be confined to the starlings."

Workhouse children

It was not only adults who ended up in the workhouse, children did too. Sometimes with one or both parents, sometimes alone. Many children were born within the workhouse walls.

In 1881 there were 183 residents (inmates) in the workhouse in Barnstaple, and 57 of them were children aged under 14. The youngest, Selina, was just two months old. The children, 26 girls and 31 boys, were from all over the Borough including Ilfracombe, Barnstaple, Marwood, Newton Tracey, Lynton, Instow, Braunton, Tawstock, Bishops Tawton, Sherwill, Swimbridge and Combe Martin[2].

Can I have some more?' Oliver Twist's naive plea has become a symbol of the harshness of workhouse life for children. The story was illustrated by George Cruikshank in 1837.

Charles Dickens, writing in the nineteenth century was very concerned about the plight of the country's poor people and his novels explored and described many aspects of life for the poor. Oliver Twist daring to ask for more gruel and being refused was part of the writer's harsh criticism of life in the workhouse for children. Dickens wrote of Oliver spending his days there 'picking oakum' - unravelling used tarred rope so that it could be rewound into useable rope. It was smelly, dirty and monotonous work, its aim not being to teach Oliver a useful skill but to keep him occupied in a way that also deterred him from ever entering a workhouse again. Life for children in the workhouse was undoubtedly harsh.

When Barnstaple Union Workhouse was first opened, the law required that young children were to be given at least three hours of education each day. This included the basics of reading, writing, arithmetic and Christian knowledge. However, the law also recognised a principle called 'less eligibility' which determined that life in the workhouse must not be better than it was for those outside. Thus, the education provided for children did not, for example, have to be as good or as comprehensive as the children might have expected (eg. from charity schools) if they had not been in the workhouse. As with Oliver Twist, outside of education hours in those early years, children were given work to do,

Children at Crumpsall workhouse in 1895

often work seen as suited to their small, nimble fingers, such as picking oakum or making delicate watch chains. The children's work made money for the Poor Law Union.

It was not until 1880 that education became compulsory for all children aged between five and ten. The Guardians duly appointed a school master and a school mistress who taught the children in a school room in the workhouse. The school master, Frederick Watts, a 20 year old man from Shirwell was school master until he was promoted to the role of Master of the workhouse in 1893.

At this point, there was discussion amongst the Guardians about whether Barnstaple should follow the lead of other Unions (375 of the other Unions it was reported) and send the children out to public schools or continue to educate them in-house. The Guardians expressed concerns that in public schools, the children would be pointed at by the other pupils and could catch diseases from them spreading epidemics. After much discussion they agreed that the older boys (aged 7 and older) would go to the Blue Coat School on North Walk and the girls

Above, Barnstaple's Blue Coat School on North Walk. Although the school has been demolished, its clock hangs on the Guildhall building, right. The Poor Law Box (page 12) is to the left of the entrance.

would go to St Mary Magdalene School on Lower Maudlin Street. The schools agreed to take the children only if they did not wear the workhouse uniform but clothes that did not give away where they lived.

At that point, no further live-in school teachers were appointed. Instead, Mr and Mrs Grubb, tailors from Mortehoe, were appointed as industrial trainers. Their focus was on training children for work.

Children went into the workhouse for many reasons. Some, living on the street, were picked up by the police or perhaps the parish priest and taken into the workhouse. These ragged children had often been abandoned by their parents.

Others went into the workhouse because of their parents' actions. For example, when a parent went into prison leaving children with no-one to look after them, or destitute parents took their children into the workhouse with them. Others were taken from their parents if they were found to be neglected or otherwise ill-treated. Some children were born in the workhouse, their mothers having taken refuge there in the later stages of their pregnancy as they had nowhere else to go.

A boy in the Blue Coat School uniform. This statue is in Exeter's Princesshay Shopping Centre near the site of Exeter's Blue Coat school

While adults could make a decision to leave the workhouse, children on their own would struggle. Perhaps their main hope was that parents or other relatives would ultimately take them in. Otherwise, children were kept in the workhouse until it was deemed possible that they would get work and somewhere to live outside.

Life was undoubtedly hard for children in the workhouse but it is likely that things did not get much easier when they left. They would have had only a basic education but also they carried with them the stigma of having been in a workhouse even though they were rarely there through any fault of their own. If children had committed a crime, reform schools were generally where they were sent, not the workhouse.

A need for change

The design of the workhouse, with separate buildings and yards, meant that children were initially kept away from the adults including members of their own families. There was a belief that the families of people in poverty were a bad influence on their children and may cause them to lead a similar life. Thus, even young children did not live with their parents in the workhouse. However, there was concern amongst the Guardians that separation was no longer taking place, perhaps largely due to overcrowding.

In 1895, the Guardians agreed that *"there ought to be a separate building for imbeciles. It was a dreadful thing that so many people quite unaccountable for their actions should be scattered about among the other inmates. There ought to be a separate ward for children."* While they agreed that the workhouse needed more separation, the Guardians decided that it would cost too much to make the House more suitable.

There were also local complaints of noise and problems in the workhouse due to the large number of young children in the building at the time. One newspaper ran with a headline of: "Troublesome babies at Barnstaple Workhouse" and reported overcrowding and noise for the other inmates and staff. At this time, many of the stories about the workhouse covered by the local papers were based on the minutes of the meetings of the Guardians of the Poor.

A short time later, there came another pressure for change. As a matter of national policy, the Government was keen to separate children from the adults, to keep them away from their bad influence and the taint of the workhouse. The Local Government Board instructed every Poor Law Union to come up with a plan for providing alternative accommodation for children.

In Barnstaple, there were 165 people in the workhouse at the time, forty of whom were children aged thirteen and under. The Guardians of the Poor were keenly aware that the Borough was not a wealthy area and that the ratepayers (those who owned land or property) would only pay so much in rates. The Guardians felt that their options for separating the children from the rest of the workhouse were limited.

For a few years, the discussion carried on between the Guardians at their fortnightly meetings with advice and cajoling coming from the Local Government Board who were keen to see change quickly.

---◆---

Ernest's Story

Rose was just 19 when she became pregnant with a man who wanted nothing more to do with her or their baby.

She was a waitress on the Quay in Ilfracombe and worked for as long as she could through the pregnancy. However, the time came when she was asked to leave her job for fear of her illegitimate pregnancy embarrassing the owners of the establishment.

Unable to afford anywhere to live, she went into the workhouse in Barnstaple. There she gave birth to a healthy baby boy who she named Ernest. She spent the first weeks with Ernest but she knew they would be separated if she kept him in there for too long. Rose's mother was in Ilfracombe and helped her get a job. She agreed to help take care of Ernest while her daughter worked even though she was working herself. So, when Ernest was just a few weeks old, Rose gratefully walked out of the workhouse with Ernest in her arms.

Tragically, Rose simply did not know how to care for her child. Unable to give him much milk as she was at work, she fed him bread to fill him up. He was found dead when he was eight weeks old. The inquest into his death was told by a doctor that Rose had done her best with the baby but his poor diet had killed him. The doctor said that the workhouse authorities should instruct every young mother leaving there about how best to feed their babies.

The Barnstaple Guardians' preferred option for removing children from the workhouse was 'boarding out'. This was an early form of fostering by which the children would be taken in by local families. The family would also receive outrelief (or outdoor relief) payments to contribute to the costs of bringing up the child. Guardians felt that this was a cheaper option than putting up new buildings or enlarging the workhouse. However, the Local Government Board was not in favour of boarding out children on this scale and said it was an option only for those children who were orphans or had been abandoned.

Instead, the Local Government wanted new accommodation for the children separate from the workhouse but still aligned to it. The Guardians looked at taking over existing buildings in Barnstaple but could not find anything suitable. They were left with the most expensive option - a new building.

In other Poor Law Unions around the country the most common solution was to build what were known as cottage homes. These comprised a number of houses, known as cottages, in which children lived with a live-in Foster Mother. She not only looked after the children but also dealt with the domestic arrangements such as cooking and cleaning. Building the workhouses in the 1830s following the formation of the Poor Law Unions was a very expensive investment for the Unions. The cottage homes was a further capital investment on a similar scale. And equally inescapable for the Barnstaple Guardians.

Finally, the Barnstaple Guardians acquiesced to the Local Government Board's way of thinking and commissioned cottage homes for children on workhouse land. There was a compromise though. Unconvinced by the need for the new homes the Barnstaple Guardians decided to have the buildings designed in such a way that they could easily be converted into residential houses should the Guardians need to sell them.

The Guardians chose to build the Homes on part of the workhouse land they already owned which reduced the cost of the venture significantly. In terms of managing the Homes into the future, the proximity of the two institutions made life much easier and more economical.

In 1901, the Local Government Board advised the Barnstaple Guardians that they did not think it desirable for them to lock down hard and fast rules for the design and management of the Cottage Homes.

Instead, they sent Herbert Preston-Thomas (pictured left), their Inspector for the South West, to help and advise the Guardians. He attended many of the Guardians' meetings in Barnstaple and gave his opinions and advice on the shaping of the Cottage Homes.

The Guardians were keen to use the services of a local builder and a local architect to keep the money in the Borough and commissioned architect William Oliver of Rock Avenue and builder William Cooke of Bear Street. William Cooke had quoted £1,816 to build the three houses, the lowest of the thirteen quotes received for the work by the Guardians.

To fund the building and furnishing costs of the Cottage Homes, the Guardians borrowed £2,200 from the Public Works Loan Commissioners. This meant that they could avoid bringing in a sudden large rates increase but instead, could spread the cost over a number of years easing the burden on the ratepayers.

Many of the cottage homes in England were built in rural areas which meant that the children could benefit from fresh air and an outdoor life away from the noise and stench of the towns. However, while the workhouse had initially been built on the very outskirts of Barnstaple and had extensive land behind it, by 1902, when the Cottage Homes were built, it was surrounded by streets of houses.

The architect of the Cottage Homes was William C Oliver, the architect of other local buildings such as the Oliver Buildings which are currently under redevelopment.

COTTAGE HOMES FOR CHILDREN

To house children previously kept in the workhouses, Welsh and English Poor Law Unions largely focused on building large 'villages' for children which were known as cottage homes, based on a model developed in Europe. They were to take children out of the workhouses from the later nineteenth century and were based on the idea that children should be brought up in isolation from the community around them.

These were huge complexes which could accommodate between 200 and 700 children. A number of 'cottages', in reality not cottages but large houses, were built typically along a private road or in a circle. Each cottage could house fifteen to forty children with a live-in foster mother to care for them. On site was a chapel, school, perhaps a swimming pool, an assembly hall, an infirmary and houses for the live-in officers such as the Master, Matron, Porter and their families. The complex would be gated to prevent the children leaving and others coming in.

There were also workshops for carpentry or shoe-making, for example, where the children could learn these skills and make items useful for the Homes. The complexes generally also had land for sports, or growing crops and raising livestock. As far as possible the cottage homes were designed to be self-sufficient so that children lived separately from the rest of the community. Visits from parents and other family members were discouraged.

A modification of the cottage homes model was developed in places such as Sheffield and Swansea, which became known as scattered homes. These were developed on the same principle of a foster mother caring for a house of children, but these 'cottages' were scattered throughout the community so they would have ordinary houses next door and the children could attend local schools and churches.

What the Barnstaple Guardians decided upon was a combination of the two models - three houses in a row on workhouse land but, unlike the 'village' model, the children were to go to local schools and churches.

With scattered homes or cottage homes in most large towns and cities, it is estimated that around 175,000[3] children spent all or part of their childhoods in these institutions in England and Wales.

Above: Aston Union Cottage Homes in north Birmingham opened in 1901 comprising 20 large houses with around 30 children in each. The workhouse was next door.

Below: Lamorbey Cottage Homes were opened in rural Sidcup for the children of the Deptford and Greenwich Poor Law Union . The workhouse itself was in Greenwich.

The opening of the Homes

The Barnstaple Homes were built between the summer of 1900 and the autumn of 1901. The buildings were then furnished and Foster Mothers appointed. Barnstaple's Cottage Homes were formally opened on Friday 18th January 1902.

This was to be a big day for the 32 children who left the workhouse and began living in the new Homes. However, there was much to happen that day before the move.

To celebrate the new Homes, the Guardians put on a Christmas party for the children of the workhouse. In the workhouse boardroom, the Guardians of the Poor took tea with the children. After the tea, the children were given presents from the Christmas tree donated by Annie Davie, the wife of the chair of the Guardians. Christmas tree parties in the workhouse boardroom had long taken place in January each year.

The vicar of St Mary's, the parish church of Barnstaple, Rev. EJ Windsor was a guest of honour along with many of the Guardians. After the party for the

The parish church that was once at the centre of the Poor Laws in the town, still stands.

The workhouse buildings (the chapel can be seen on the left) were opposite the new Cottage Homes. Photo reproduced here with the kind permission of Susan Pengelly.

children, there were speeches. The vicar of St Mary's remarked on the kindness shown by George and Annie Davie, the chair of the Guardians and his wife, and expressed his hope that the children would be happy in their new quarters. When George Davie spoke, he talked directly to the children. He said they should remember the kindnesses that had been shown to them by the Master and Matron of the workhouse, Frederick and Selina Watts, and that he hoped they would be good in their homes and give the Foster Mothers as little trouble as possible. He hoped they would grow up to be good men and women. He then observed that a great deal of responsibility rested on the Foster Mothers who were going to be an example to the children.

The 32 children then left the workhouse and walked the short distance across to the new buildings. William Cooke, the builder, was there waiting and presented each child with a parcel containing half a pound of nuts, half a pound of sweets and some oranges.

The new cottages were two storey brick houses, approximately 33 feet wide, with several windows and glass panels in the doors, to make the most of any daylight. The change of scale would have been very noticeable to the children in comparison with the large rooms and passageways of the workhouse.

The children were taken into each cottage through an arched doorway which opened onto a hallway. On the ground floor, they would have seen a large dining room with a wooden floor. There was also a kitchen and a bathroom with three toilets and four basins. Each basin had hot and cold water. There was also a storeroom, scullery, and a larder. Oil lamps around the rooms gave light on this wintery evening. There was a coal house, essential as coal was the fuel which heated the water and the rooms.

Upstairs, there were two dormitories with wooden floors. With only 32 children going in on this first day, there was plenty of space. There was a bathroom with a bath, slop sinks, drying closets and toilets, and also on this floor were the living quarters for the Foster Mother. With her room being between the dormitories, she was able to keep an eye on all the children at nighttime.

Once the Guardians had gone home and the children were settled in their individual cottages, the primary difference from the workhouse would no doubt have been the relatively few people around — only a dozen children and just one adult, the Foster Mother, in each cottage. Once she put out the oil lamp in the dormitory and tiptoed out to her own room, there may have been a quietness that the children were just not used to. The following morning, as well as exploring the house with the benefit of daylight, the children also got to see the yards at the back of each house. These were stone and earth underfoot with brick walls around. The Foster Mother could see the children playing there through the windows of the cottage.

At the front of the cottages, the glass in the windows downstairs was frosted so the children did not have, from the inside, a view of the road and the workhouse beyond although they could see it clearly from the upstairs windows.

The first children in the Homes

Of the 32 children who walked into the Homes that January evening, there were nineteen girls aged between four and twelve years old and twelve boys aged between four and thirteen. Eleven of the children had been in the workhouse with their mothers and so the move to the Cottage Homes meant leaving them behind. Most of the children, twenty-two, were with siblings. Eight had been in the workhouse with no relatives with them at all.

Henry who was three, had been in the workhouse with his older sister Winifred who was five, his younger sister who was just a year old and their mother, a twenty six year old charwoman from Ilfracombe. She was not married and probably had little hope of bringing up her family on a charwoman's pay alone.

Alfred and Lucy from Barnstaple had no parents in the workhouse but had been sent there by themselves. He was ten and sister was seven.

Violet was just three years old when she went in to the Cottage Homes. She was a child on her own with no parents or siblings in the workhouse.

To be away from the noise, smells and people of the workhouse may have been a relief to them. For those with a mother in the workhouse, saying goodbye must have been painful. But the Foster Mothers were intended to provide a homely or feminine touch to the children's lives to bring them some comfort and guidance. Having a yard to run around in was no doubt a treat even in the cold air of January.

The older children also had significant freedoms. They were to go to local schools and the local church which would mean walking in Barnstaple, seeing other people and mixing with people in the local community.

In other ways, things for the children would have remained very similar to the workhouse - the house ran to a strict timetable with times for getting up and going to bed set in stone, meals were decided for them and held at set times. Opportunities for being fussy about what you ate, or having snacks, did not exist. The children ate what was put in front of them or they didn't eat at all.

With around 170 people living in the workhouse, plus staff, the building was a noisy, smelly, active place. By contrast, the only adults in the Cottage Homes were the Foster Mothers. With 32 children, it is unlikely to have been quiet often in the Cottage Homes, but it may have been a more manageable environment for many of the children. Behind the cottages was a collar factory and a saw mill. These too were noisy places with comings and goings behind the walls of the children's yards.

Cottage 1 was generally for boys, cottage 3 for girls and the cottage in the middle was often mixed, depending on who the Cottage Homes were accommodating at the time. The yard of Cottage 1 was particularly small, as the yards and sheds of the houses backing onto it from on Azes Road ate into the space.

---❖---

Amy and Ethel's Story

Two of the girls who went into the Cottage Homes that first evening were Amy and Ethel, aged twelve and eight respectively. They had been living in Lynton with their parents and three siblings but the children and their mother came into the workhouse when Ethel was just a baby. Despite being in a job, and reportedly earning 18 shillings a week, their father had not paid any maintenance for the family's time in the workhouse. Consequently, he was sent to prison. By the time the Cottage Homes were opened, Amy and Ethel's older siblings had left the workhouse to go into live-in domestic service jobs known as 'situations'. The two remaining girls, however, left their mother still in the workhouse when they walked over to the Cottage Homes that day.

The country prison was in Exeter and there were strong links between the Exeter Gaol and Barnstaple Workhouse as some of the children had family members there and many of the inmates were sent there if they were found to have broken the workhouse rules by refusing to work or absconding, for example.

Picture courtesy of www.exetermemories.co.uk

The early years

Although the children's Cottage Homes were in separate buildings from the workhouse the two were run on very similar, intertwined ways. The Master of the workhouse, Frederick Watts, was also appointed as the Superintendent of the Cottage Homes; he simply added tasks relating to the Cottage Homes into his daily routine.

The Guardians met every two weeks to discuss both the Homes and the House. The meetings were held in the boardroom of the workhouse which had been built specially for this purpose in 1895 and could seat 80 people. It had its own passageway from the workhouse entrance so that the Guardians did not have to go through the main workhouse building to reach it. The faces of previous Guardians stared down on them from portraits on the walls. At times such as Christmas, the children of the Cottage Homes would gather in the boardroom for a party.

For the children, however, it is unlikely that they were aware of the links with the workhouse. Aside from the physical proximity of the building, and their Christmas visits, their lives were separate from it and all those who lived inside.

───────❖───────

James's Story

In October 1904. James's mother was found guilty of theft. The prosecution said that she had 14 prior convictions dating back as far as 1887. She was sentenced to 12 months in Exeter Prison and James was sent to the Barnstaple Cottage Homes.

In the following September, James' mother wrote to the Guardians asking to have James back when she had completed her sentence. The Guardians discussed the case, and heard a report from the NSPCC who felt that the best place for the child was an industrial school. The Guardians decided, given the criminal record of his mother, that they should take responsibility for him until he was 18. In an act intended to protect him from the criminal taint of his mother, they duly sent him to an industrial school. These schools were harsh places in which children worked for their keep and had a disciplined existence with few freedoms. Industrial schools carried a terrible stigma, and children who had spent time there often found it difficult to get work or to be accepted into society in adulthood.

The Foster Mothers

When the Cottage Homes idea was developed, it was widely considered that the best people to look after these cottages of children were women. It was considered best for their commitment to the job if they were single women with no children of their own to distract them although the hours of the job were such that there was really no possibility of such distractions. They were to live in the cottages and be there twenty-four hours a day, seven days a week, to meet the care needs of the fifteen or so children living in their cottage. There were no weekends, and no evenings out. There was never even a suggestion that a man could be considered for the role.

This is an incredible commitment to ask of young women who had not yet established a family of their own. And yet it was primarily their care, skills and human touch that could make the difference between a good childhood for each of the children in her care or a terrible one. Aside from teachers in the local school, the Foster Mothers would be the only adults with whom the children would have a day-to-day relationship.

As they would be with the Foster Mother, in most circumstances, until they were around 14 years old, the relationship with the foster mother was critical to their well-being and yet the Foster Mothers largely had no prior experience of looking after children, were given no training and had very little support, monitoring or supervision in what must have been a very difficult job at times.

The Foster Mothers were responsible for cleaning, making and mending the children's clothes, preparing the meals as well as ensuring the children were clean, kept occupied and out of trouble, and attended school each day.

BARUM WORKHOIUSE
1902: A mystery

Just a few months after the Cottage Homes had opened, there were two tragic unexplained deaths in the workhouse. A 30 year old woman and her son Stephen died in the House within just six days of each other. Stephen was only eleven months old. What could have caused mother and her baby son to have died together in the workhouse? The deaths were not recorded as having been discussed in the Guardians' meetings.

The first advert for Foster Mothers appeared in the local paper in October 1901 while the finishing touches to the new Cottage Homes were being carried out. It is interesting that the advert requested knowledge of bringing up children and yet asked that applicants had no family.

BARNSTAPLE UNION
THREE FOSTER MOTHERS WANTED.

T HE GUARDIANS of the Barnstaple Union INVITE APPLICATIONS for the appointment of THREE FOSTERS MOTHERS for their Cottage Homes at Barnstaple.

Applicants must be single women or widows without family, and will have a knowledge of the care and bringing up of children.

Salary £20 per annum, with furnished apartments and rations.

Applications in the handwriting of the candidates, with copies of three testimonials of recent date, stating age, previous and present occupation, must reach me no later than Thursday the 21st inst.

By order of the Board, W. H. TOLLER, CLERK

Barnstaple, 5th November, 1901

An advert placed for Foster Mothers before the Homes opened.
In 1908 'good needle woman' was added to the requirements of the position.

Four applications were received for the jobs. The Guardians decided to appoint three of the four – Miss Viney, Miss Reece and Mrs Squire.

All three women were from Barnstaple, in their mid thirties and none were married, Mrs Squire's husband having died a few years earlier. Miss Reece was working as a nurse before her appointment and so had very useful skills for her new role in the Homes. Only Mrs Squire had children of her own, the youngest of whom was five years old. Who did her children live with while she was living with other people's children in the Cottage Homes? With only an occasional afternoon off permitted for each Foster Mother, she would have seen her children only very rarely.

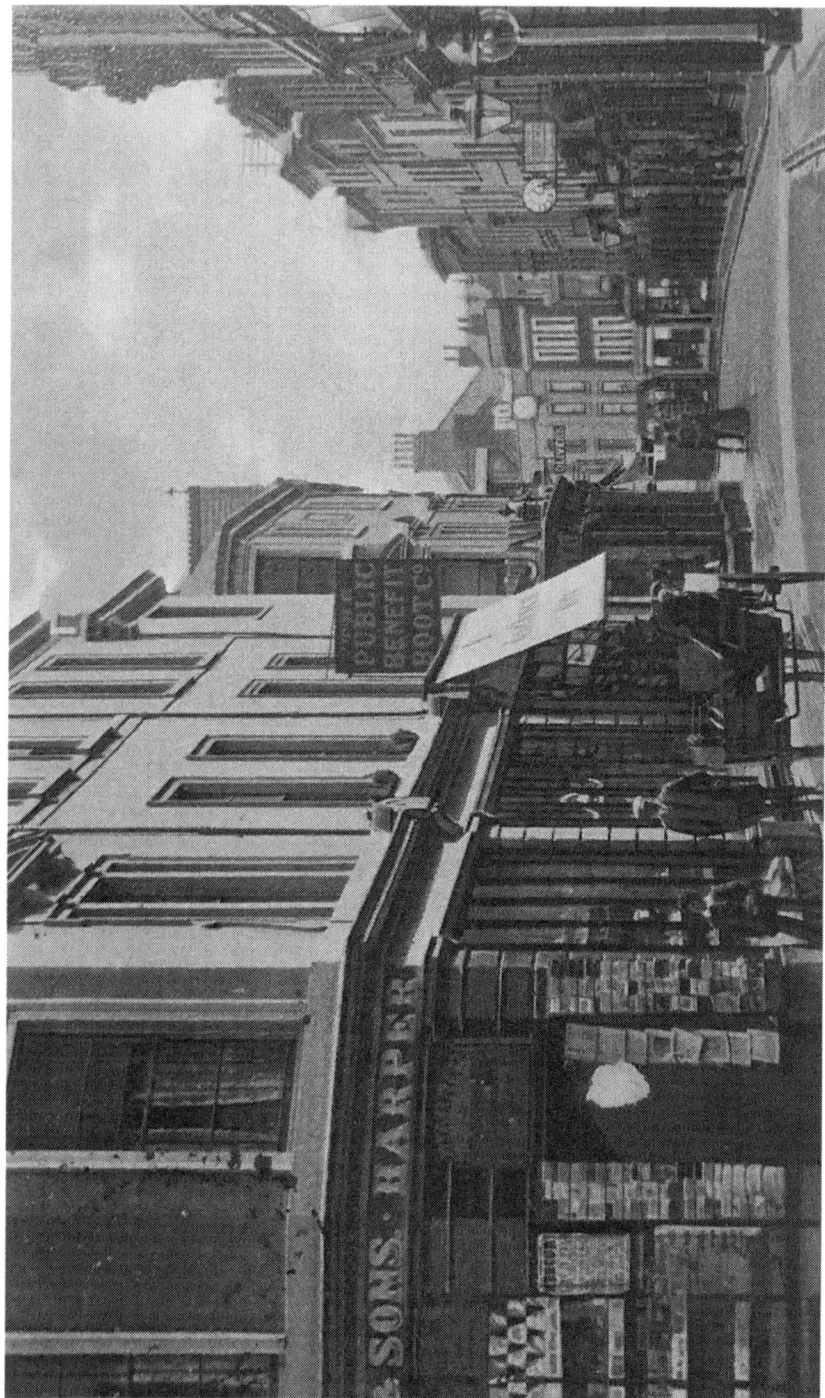

Barnstaple High Street in around 1906

Agnes's Story

Agnes was born in Barnstaple Union Workhouse and was four when the Cottage Homes opened. The opening ceremony will have meant little to her at that age but leaving her mother behind in the workhouse no doubt felt a very significant loss to her.

Her mother was described as being 'feeble-minded'. As such, the Guardians took responsibility for Agnes and found her a family to be boarded out (fostered) with. After she had finished school, Agnes stayed with the family as a domestic servant.

Agnes's mother remained in the workhouse and died there 33 years after her daughter had been born there.

After just a few months as a Foster Mother, Miss Reece became ill. She was granted two weeks leave of absence and went into Ilfracombe Cottage Hospital (on the site of what is now the Tyrell). After three weeks, the clerk reported to the Guardians that she had not returned to work and that her health "was completely broken down". The Guardians said that because of this, she would be given formal notice that her contract would be terminated on 25th December. Without a Foster Mother in place, her cottage was closed and the children living there were moved into the other two cottages.

Miss Reece wrote to the Guardians to say that she was upset at losing her job and that she was actually getting stronger and would be able to start work again soon. The Guardians disagreed and appointed a new Foster Mother.

There is no doubt that the Foster Mothers had a challenging role, single-handedly looking after fifteen children, more at times. The children covered a full range of ages and some had disabilities and illnesses warranting particular care and attention. One of the primary challenges was that the Foster Mothers had very little time off. They had children in their care for 24 hours a day – older children went off to school during the day but they still had the youngest and those who were sick to look after. They were permitted only occasional afternoons off. In 1903, however, it was agreed that they could have two weeks a year leave of absence for a holiday.

The workhouse and the Cottage Homes were visited annually by an inspector from the Local Government Board. At the inspection visit towards the end of 1904, the inspector raised a problem with the Foster Mothers. In his view, they were spending most of their time simply trying to keep up with the washing generated by 45 children and three adults and had little time for anything else. The only tools they had to help them were a hand-powered washer with a handle to turn the clothes in soapy water, and a hand-turned mangle to squeeze the water out. In 1906, to ease the burden, an assistant Foster Mother was appointed for one day a week to help out with the washing.

---❖---

Ethel's Story

Fifteen year old Ethel's mother was blind and her father was a farm labourer bringing into the family only limited earnings. He described Ethel as 'feeble-minded', a description given to people with learning disabilities. This is likely to have to have prevented her getting work. As the children in labourers' families needed to start bringing money into the family as soon as they were old enough, this would have been a significant problem for Ethel's father. In a pleading letter to the Guardians, he said that he could no longer look after Ethel, as well as his wife and his two younger daughters. The Guardians accepted his plea and Ethel was taken into their care. Six years later, and now aged 21, Ethel was still living in the workhouse.

BARUM WORKHOUSE
1904: Reducing the stigma

In 1904, the Registrar General said that all workhouses should remove any reference to the workhouse on the birth certificates of those who were born in the institution. The Barnstaple Guardians chose to refer to the House as 19 Alexandra Road instead. It was hoped that this would remove the shame that existed for those who began life in the workhouse. In 1919, it was decided that this would also apply to death certificates for those whose lives ended in the workhouse or in the Cottage Homes.

THE SUPERINTENDENT

Frederick Watts had a long career in the workhouse and saw many changes. Having been brought up in Shirwell, he first started working in the Workhouse as a twenty year old in 1879. He was appointed as the school master and had rooms in the workhouse building. Twelve years later, he married Selina from Goodleigh and she moved into his rooms.

He was appointed Master of the workhouse in 1893 and Selina, as his wife, was appointed Matron. It was not unusual in workhouses and cottage homes for appointments to be made to couples, based primarily (although not always exclusively) on the man's attributes for the job.

In 1899,the couple's son was born and he spent his entire childhood living with them in the workhouse building. The couple's two other children both died when they were infants.

When the Cottage Homes opened in 1902, Frederick was given the additional role of Superintendent of them with a substantial additional salary awarded. He saw this as primarily an accounting role and kept careful records of all expenditure and reported these to the Guardians along with any other issues which needed their consideration.

There are few contemporary depictions of workhouse masters. This is an illustration of Mr and Mrs Bumble, the fictional Master and Matron of the workhouse where Oliver Twist was. There is evidence that were cats in Barnstaple workhouse as well as in this fictional sitting room.

Going to School

The school leaving age when the Homes were opened was twelve and, as the Guardians had decided not to build Cottage Homes with their own school room and teacher, the children were sent out to local schools from the age of five years old. The problem was always going to be finding enough places in local schools to absorb the influx of around thirty Cottage Homes children when the Homes first opened.

Initially, they were split between three schools - Bear Street School; the Wesleyan school on Reform Street and the St Mary Magdalene School on Lower Maudlin Street[4].

Reform Street and St Mary Magdalene School were both north of the Homes, near Vicarage Street. While the Bear Street School was around a five minute walk from the Homes, it may have taken a further ten minutes to reach St Mary Magdalene School. The older children would have helped walking the younger children to their schools.

It was not all plain sailing. The headmasters sometimes wrote to the Guardians to complain that a child was misbehaving or had arrived late, presumably in much the same fashion as they would have written to another child's parents if there were problems at school. Absenteeism was, at times, a problem amongst the Homes children. On one occasion, the Guardians received a letter from the headmaster of St Mary Magdalene's School saying that a boy from the Cottage Homes had been absent. When they asked the Foster Mother about it, it surmised that she had kept him back to clean the stairs as a punishment for some other wrongdoing.

———————❖———————

Alice's Story

Alice was taken into the workhouse in the 1890s as a young girl. Some years later, as a fourteen year old in the Cottage Homes, the Guardians were considering her future. She had lost one arm and so the Guardians were concerned that it may not be easy to find an employer who would give her the support she would need to do her work. Interestingly, the Superintendent of the Homes, Frederick Watts, had also lost a limb. He had just one hand but this had not stopped from having a successful working life. However, the Guardians resolved to find Alice a suitable institution to go into. They contacted the National Children's Homes in London but they warned they had a long waiting list. In fact, it was two and half years before she was given a place at the Chipping Norton branch where she was to assist the Sister-in-charge with looking after the children. She set off by train in January 1990.

However, after a little over a month, the Children's Homes said that she must return to the workhouse as the placement was not suitable. She was put in the Ladies' Carriage of the Barnstaple train leaving Paddington at 10.30am. That autumn, however, there was to be good news for Alice. Her sister had said that she could go and stay with her in Bristol if the Guardians would allow it. Alice was eighteen by this time. She got work in domestic service and in later life she married.

In 1906, a new school for Barnstaple children opened on Ashleigh Road. Attending this school would mean a shorter walk for the children from the Cottage Homes and so the Guardians were determined that this was the school for them. A shorter walk, they felt, was likely to reduce absenteeism.

Unfortunately, the Department of Education had other plans for the new school. It was a large school, having places for 310 children, but, much to the annoyance of the Guardians, the places were filled immediately by taking in the pupils of two existing schools which were due to close - Newport Church School and the Grosvenor Street School. A long argument broke out. Because communication was by letters, discussions with outside agencies always took a long time. Each time a letter was received from the headmaster, the clerk would read it out at the next Guardians' meeting, the Guardians would discuss how to respond, vote on it, the clerk would be charged with writing a letter in response and then they would wait to receive the reply. Each time, the awaited reply turned out to be a stubborn refusal to accept any more pupils. The Guardians threatened to take Cottage Homes children to the door of the school and see if the headmaster would turn them away. In January 1907, after several weeks of letter-writing, they did just that. A boy called Freddie was taken to the school gates where the headmaster met him and promptly sent him away.

The Guardians sent another angry letter. This time, they had more success. Freddie had disabilities and the Guardians' argued that he needed to go to a school closer to the Homes because of his difficulties walking. It turned out that this was an impossible argument to counter and so eight year old Freddie was allowed to attend Ashleigh Road School. The Guardians were to write many more letters about Freddie over the next decade More of this later.

All the other children were sent, from this time, to St Mary Magdalene School which was a National School for children of all ages. This meant that all the children could walk to the school together. With the exception of Freddie of course who continued to go to Ashleigh Road School.

The children's diet

The kitchens were not large in the Homes so much of the meal preparation was carried out in the workhouse where a cook and helpers were employed and the kitchen was equipped for large-scale meal preparation. There was good storage space in the workhouse so supplies could be kept easily. There were also economies of scale to be achieved by both institutions buying the same food and other items from the same suppliers.

The food was plain and simple with lots of filling food such as bread, dumplings cake and porridge. In normal circumstances, the children in the Homes (and the inmates of the workhouse) were fed according to a dietary table that was submitted periodically by the Local Government Board. The table aimed to ensure that the children were eating properly in an economical fashion. It was down to the Guardians to source local suppliers of the food.

The dietary tables had to be very strictly adhered to by the Barnstaple Guardians and even minor changes were not allowed. For example, several times the Guardians requested that they be able to give the children scalded milk instead of raw milk. The scalding process heated the milk and meant that it lasted longer and was cheaper to buy. And several times, the Local Government Board wrote back to say there was absolutely no way that this was acceptable even though it was the cheaper and more practical option.

On one occasion, the Guardians were admonished for the children being given tea on Wednesday evenings when according to the dietary tables, it should have been cocoa. Additionally, the children had been given three quarters of a pint of broth for Monday's dinner instead of the half pint that was scheduled. The Guardians had to ensure that such a diversion from the written plan did not occur again.

The weekly meal plan:

Sundays—bread and milk for breakfast; beef, vegetables and bread for dinner; bread and butter and cocoa for supper

Mondays—bread and butter and tea for breakfast; broth, bread and cheese and dumplings for dinner; and bread and milk for supper

Tuesday—porridge with milk and sugar added for breakfast, bacon, vegetables, and sultana puddings for dinner; bread and milk for supper

Wednesdays—bread and milk for breakfast, Irish stew for dinner; bread and butter and cocoa for supper

Thursdays—bread and butter and cocoa for breakfast; fish, potatoes and bread for dinner; bread and milk for supper.

Fridays—bread and milk for breakfast; boiled mutton, bread and vegetables and rice pudding for dinner; bread and butter and cocoa for supper

Saturdays—porridge for breakfast, soup for dinner, bread and milk for supper

Every day the children had cake for lunch.

———————❖———————

Wilfrid and his siblings

In around 1907, Mr D left his family in Barnstaple and went to Wales to find work. His wife and five children were left without any means of taking care of themselves so Mrs D took herself and her five children into the workhouse. The eldest child was 14, the youngest only a baby. When she later left the workhouse, she took the baby with her but left her other children.

The Guardians wrote to Mr D in Wales to tell him to contribute towards the costs of his children in the Cottage Homes. He wrote back enclosing a postal order for 10 shillings and querying how many children he had in the Homes. The letter created newspaper headlines such as:

"Barnstaple Man Forgot How Many Children He Has"

There was a tragedy behind the mocking headline, however. The Guardians wrote back to him revealing that, just weeks before, his eldest child had died in the workhouse.

The letters continued back and forth. The Guardians needed him to pay for his three remaining children, he said he could not afford it and he couldn't take them as he was in lodgings. In the following October, he was sentenced to a month in prison with hard labour for the failure to pay. Tragically, in 1911, his daughter Gladys and son Wilfrid were still in the Cottage Homes and a few years later, he himself, now in his sixties, went into Barnstaple Workhouse.

BARUM WORKHOUSE
1909: A pleading letter

"Honourable sir.

"For nearly 12 years I was in the civil service which I left on November 20th 1890 without pension.

"I never learnt any trade and during the past 7 or 8 years I have had no regular employment, consequently have been on several occasions an inmate of Barnstaple Workhouse. My age is 52 years. Last year I got an order for the House with an understanding I was to have no leave. As the only place for recreation is a small yard closely surrounded by the bricks of dwelling houses to say nothing about the WC, urinal, donkey house, dead house, ash pit &c adjoining, there is no chance of getting fresh air and after being confined for months together I became very nervous and ill and for that reason I was compelled to take my discharge on 27th August last.

"As I could get no employment and being absolutely destitute I again applied to the Barnstaple Guardians on the 5th and 9th ultimo for another order which was refused on both occasions.

"Since my discharge I have been 6 times in the Tramp Ward and 4 times I have walked about all night. I have no wish to do anything wrong or break the law, neither do I wish to fly in the face of authority but I am altogether at a loss to know what to do under the circumstances, therefore I should esteem it a very great favour if you would kindly condescend to inform me how to act.

Sincerely apologising for troubling you, I am honourable sir your humble obedient servant."

Sgd Charles B_____

The Guardians took walking out of the workhouse very seriously and did not appreciate people changing their minds. However, after more begging letters, Charles was eventually readmitted into Barnstaple Workhouse where he died 18 months later.

The first decade of the Cottage Homes was a time of settling in. Many changes were made to the Cottage Homes as the Guardians learnt more about what was needed. The internal layout of the Homes was altered significantly to include isolation and sick rooms. In 1906 the yards were asphalted and, in 1909, electric lights were installed bringing brightness into the oil lamp gloom. The Guardians were also offered a telephone service, but they didn't feel there was a need.

After the sacking of one Foster Mother in 1909, the Guardians issued changes to the rules of the Homes which were intended to give more control to the Superintendent and take some control away from the Foster Mothers. In addition, the Foster Mothers were told that they had to sit with the children at mealtimes and that the doors to the Homes were to be closed at 10pm. The Guardians did not record why these modifications to the rules were necessary.

There were a lot of changes in terms of who the three Foster Mothers were as new women arrived and others left. A relief Foster Mother was appointed in 1906 to cover times when the foster mothers were granted leave.

In the space of less than two years, two foster mothers fell seriously ill with blood poisoning. The first said it was the result of pricking her finger with a darning needle, the second said that she had sustained a scratch or prick to a finger which became septic. The women complained to the Guardians who made claims on their insurance. In both cases, the insurance company said that there was no proof the injuries had taken place as a result of the work but were happy to make a small payment towards the medical bills even though there was no legal liability. The first Foster Mother was too ill to work for several weeks and the Guardians asked her to resign so that they could appoint someone else. The second woman recovered but resigned of her own accord soon afterwards.

BARUM WORKHOUSE
1911: A workhouse suicide

Tragically Elias, an inmate, was found in the workhouse with his throat cut and died within a hour of being found. An inquest into his death heard that the 38 year had previously been working as a driver in Braunton but he had been admitted to the Workhouse on Saturday. At around 2am on the following Tuesday morning he had rushed out of bed. He went over to the mantel shelf where he took a piece of broken mirror that was lying there and inflicted the fatal wound.

---❖---

Florry's story

In 1913, Florry's aunt wrote to the Guardians asking if her niece, then aged thirteen and living in the Cottage Homes, could go and live with her in Tiverton. She said she wanted her to help in the kitchen and would give her a good home. One of the Guardians said that he had seen the aunt's premises and that it was more of an eating house than a public house. He said that she and her husband were respectable and would give her time to attend church and Sunday School. The Guardians agreed to Florry going to live there.

After just eighteen months however Florry was returned to the Cottage Homes, her aunt saying that she could no longer stay with her. In better news, Florry was later taken in by her grandparents.

Through these early years there was no question of the Cottage Homes becoming independent of the Barnstaple Workhouse as happened in some other Unions. Instead, the bond remained tight with a single Visiting Committee (comprising members of the Board of Guardians) taking the bulk of the responsibility for monitoring and reporting on both the Cottage Homes and workhouse. This joint approach was to prove very useful in terms of coping with the impacts of the Great War.

The boys of the Homes wore the workhouse uniform of caps, corduroy trousers and cotton or flannel shirts with beige dresses and pinafores for the girls. Both wore woollen stockings with unnailed shoes or strong nailed boots.

The Great War

In 1914 there were four cases of scarlet fever in the Homes which turned out to be mild although warranted the appointment of a temporary nurse to care for the children. In May, the children were taken on their first motor car trip. The year was to take a very different turn, however.

While the horrors of the Great War developed, the role of the Cottage Homes became even more important. Whole families were devastated by the effects of war and many thousands of children were left orphaned or in poverty. Throughout the country, the need to look after these children was critical.

The Cottage Homes were full of children and the workhouse full of individuals and families who could no longer afford to feed themselves, women who struggled to maintain their families on their own, the elderly or infirm who longer had anyone to look after them and others displaced by the war.

The Guardians were busy trying to provide indoor and outdoor relief for a growing number and range of need in the Borough with limited funding. However, the more pressing problem, as the War went on, became how to continue to feed, clothe, and keep warm those in the Homes and the workhouse and how to continue to staff the institutions.

War brought shortages of even the most basic of foods and price rises affected nearly all the Guardian's

The War Memorial in Barnstaple

purchases. Tea was an early issue with the Guardians finding that there were great difficulties finding tea to buy although it was one of the staple drinks of the children. Fish also became difficult to source and all grocery prices generally increased significantly. As time went on shortages were not simply a question of economics but it was considered a duty to the country to be as sparing as possible with some foods. A letter from the Local Government Board in 1915 impressed on the Guardians the urgent need for strict economy in every branch of the Union's expenditure whether capital or revenue.

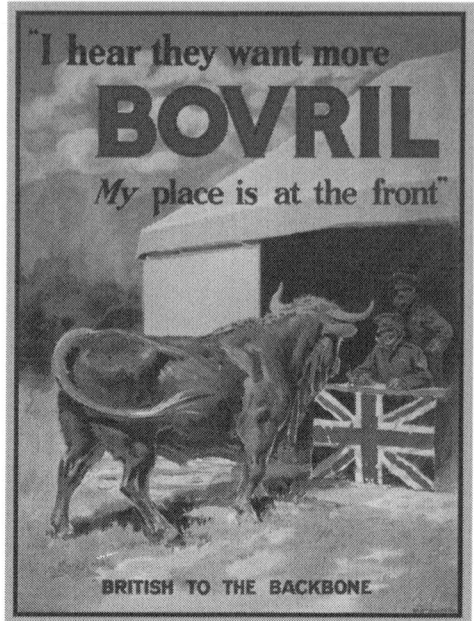

Bovril was a common drink in workhouses and was also served to the children in Barnstaple's Cottage Homes, along with cod liver oil which was also though to be healthy.

Coal was a very difficult problem for the Homes and the House as it was the only source of power for heating, hot water and cooking. The Guardians had to pay far more for supplies while attempts were made to use it economically.

The Local Government Board wrote to ask all Guardians to ensure in their institutions that extra potatoes and other vegetables were used in soups and stews instead of beef and that, three evenings a week, jam was used to be used instead of butter or margarine on bread.

Soon after, the Local Government Board also requested that there should be frugal use of the blankets as there was a national shortage of wool. Not ideal at a time when coal was also in short supply.

People with medical qualifications were particularly needed in the war effort and they were specifically asked to prepare themselves for being called up. Barnstaple Union had two doctors called up in such a way which made providing medical services for the Homes, the House and people still in their own homes very difficult. The remaining Medical Officers had to take on far more visiting duties.

A widower

Not all children in need could be taken in by the Cottage Homes. For example, in 1916, the Guardians were asked to consider the case of Mr G of Pilton whose wife had died a few months earlier leaving him with their four children to look after. The oldest was ten, the youngest three years old. In his letter, Mr G said he was a laundry man earning 25/- a week. For each of the three children he said, he would pay the Guardians maintenance of 2 shillings a week.

The Guardians considered his case and wrote back to him saying they would not take his children. Mr G, however, did well. Sharing somewhere to live with another family meant he was able to have someone there to look after the children while he continued to work. In this way, he was able to keep his family together.

In 1918, only months before the end of the war, the Local Government Board sent out a letter requesting Unions provide any waste paper which could be re-pulped to make more. The Chair of the Guardians, William T Buckingham, said that the Union had a "considerable quantity of useless books" and the clerk was told to "dispose of all the old books and papers which in his opinion were no longer of use to the Union".

The Barnstaple Guardians were, aside from losing a couple of the medical officers and the longstanding chair of the Guardians having to resign due to ill health in 1916, relatively fortunate in the staff they kept on during the war. The Superintendent and Matron, for example were there throughout as were the three Foster Mothers: Mrs Hoare from Hartland, Mrs Short from Barnstaple and Miss Huxtable from Goodleigh. After many changes of Foster Mothers throughout the first decade of the Homes, Mrs Hoare was appointed in 1909, Miss Huxtable in 1910 and Mrs Short in 1915 and they all stayed in post until long after the war was over.

Peace celebrations

While the end of the War did not bring about an immediate end to the problems of sourcing and paying for essential items, there was a determination in Barnstaple to celebrate peace and this was also true of the workhouse and the Cottage Homes.

The Guardians planned a special tea for all of those in the workhouse and in the Cottage Homes. Unfortunately, on the morning of the meal, the ordered vegetables failed to arrive. Local people stepped in to help and picked what they could from their allotments. Very soon, the Guardians had everything they needed and more. The celebration meal could go ahead. Workhouse inmates were given an extra day's leave of absence and were entertained in the market by the town's Mayor, Frank Jewell. Those unable to be there had their teas sent to them. The Mayor and Mayoress organised a concert in the boardroom for all the residents of the House and the Homes.

Frederick Watts, the Master of the workhouse and Superintendent of the Home resigned in 1919, largely, he said, because of the impact of the war itself. When he resigned, he explained how hard the job had been for him and his wife in recent years: "Matron, without being employed to do so, has cut out and made or supervised the making and repairing of the whole of the female's clothing as well as the men's inside clothing and the bedding. On account of the rationing etc. caused by the war we have had no holidays since 1916 and the strain and worry of the last few years has been so acute that we feel it absolutely impossible to continue in office."

He had been the Master for 26 years meaning that his character and personality and the influence of his wife would have had a significant impact on the character of the workhouse and the lives of its inmates. The chair of the Guardians described him as a "strict disciplinarian".

After leaving Barnstaple Workhouse, the couple became Master and Matron at Torrington Workhouse on a temporary basis.

Frank and Gertrude George replaced them at Barnstaple Workhouse. They were the first Master and Matron to have had previous experience of the roles, having been Master and Matron at Cerne Abbas in Dorset. Like the previous Master and Matron, they had children of their own who lived with them in the workhouse.

Sadly, Frederick Watts died just four years after his resignation. He had moved back to Barnstaple and he and his wife were living close to the Cottage Homes when he died peacefully sitting in his armchair.

Some problems in the Homes

The Guardians held their meetings in private, with only Guardians actively taking part. While these were closed meetings, the issues under discussion and conversations that had taken place were reported to the local papers as well as being recorded in the minutes book. While some topics were recorded in detail, others were not as if perhaps the Guardians were careful that not everything should be in the public eye. For example, two Foster Mothers were sacked but no reasons were given in the minutes, despite the second sacking giving rise to a change in some ways of working in the Homes.

However, in the following years, with Frank George as Master, there were signs of what was perhaps greater openness. This brought indications in the minutes and press reports that not all was well in the House and Homes.

BARUM WORKHOUSE
Ada's story

Ada went into the workhouse with her young son and daughter. Her children were placed into the Cottage Homes leaving their mother in the Workhouse.

Four years after arriving in the Workhouse, when she was 37, her son was eight and her daughter was six, she was found very unwell in the bathroom of the Workhouse by another inmate. Ada had been cleaning for the Matron using carbolic acid (commonly used as a cleaning disinfectant) when it was realised that she was missing.

The Master went to see her immediately and thought it was clear that she had deliberately swallowed some of the carbolic fluid. She was very ill for a time but later recovered. Attempting to kill yourself was illegal so she was arrested and put on trial. In court, she did not deny what had happened and said she was "tired of her life". Asked if she was going to try it again she answered "certainly not". Frederick Watts, As the Master, spoke well of her to the court. She was he was found guilty, but bound over, and returned to the Workhouse.

Her children spent their entire childhoods in the Homes and she was in there for most of her adult life, dying in the House aged 65.

In 1919, it was discussed that local children were frequently climbing on the sheds at the back of the cottages, peering through the windows of the Homes, shouting, and throwing stones and other things into the yards. This must have been concerning and perhaps distressing for the children and the Foster Mothers. Was it also an indication of how they were treated on the streets, at school and in the parks?

Additionally there was increasing dissatisfaction reported amongst the staff, particularly the Foster Mothers, about their level of pay. Despite the passage of time, the Foster Mothers were being paid only £1 more a year than they were when the Cottage Homes first opened in 1902 - £21 a year plus accommodation in the Cottage Homes and rations.

The three Foster Mothers together asked the Guardians for an increase of salary. They said that what they were being paid was "not at all sufficient having regard to the responsibility and work entailed". The Guardians considered the matter and said no.

Interestingly, the 1919 Report from the Ministry of Health's inspector, Mr Court, said that "he always thought that in North Devon, they were paying lower salaries than the average". Over the following years, the salaries of all the staff involved in indoor relief in Barnstaple were increased.

---------------❖---------------

John's story

John went into Barnstaple Workhouse as an infant leaving his parents and siblings in the family home. His father was an unskilled labourer bringing in a small income. His brothers became nurserymen and his sister worked as a domestic servant. John was categorised as an 'imbecile' and it seems he never left the workhouse. The issue of finding places to live for people in the Cottage Homes who had disabilities or mental illness appears to have been an ongoing problem for the Guardians. Many children were simply sent over to live out their lives in the workhouse, Sadly, John was such a child. He never returned to live with his family.

In 1909, his mother died. Three years later, John also died. He was aged just 26.

Paying for the children

The Guardians of the Poor were very concerned about the cost of the Homes. The primary function of their fortnightly meetings was to look at the accounts which were kept by the Master of the workhouse. They looked at every item of expenditure, the largest being the repayment of the loan taken out to build the Cottage Homes, down to the smallest measure of salt. For every item to be bought in, and every item of work that needed doing in terms of the maintenance of the buildings, the Guardians would advertise for tenders from local people and then select the lowest local bid.

These expenses they reconciled against the money coming in, primarily the poor rates paid by the local ratepayers. Barnstaple Guardians were always concerned that the burden on the ratepayers should be kept as low as possible.

Another source of income was the amount people would pay for their children to be kept in the Homes. When any child came into the Homes, the Guardians had to seek out the person liable for contributing to the costs of their maintenance. Some, such as orphans, had their stay entirely funded through poor rates, others had parents who were found to be liable to make a regular contribution because it was felt that they had sufficient potential earning power to be able to afford it.

Lone mothers were generally not expected to be able fund their child's stay. Fathers, on the other hand, unless disabled or infirm, were legally obliged to make a contribution whether they were lone parents or married.

However, if an illegitimate or widowed mother was found to have married, the new husband took on the financial liability of his wife's child.

─────── ❖ ───────

William's Story

Twelve year old William in was taken into the Homes in January 1911. At a Guardians meeting a few days later, it was decided that William's mother's husband be sent a a letter informing him that he must remove William from the Homes as there was no arrangement for maintenance to be paid for him. William's stepfather wrote back saying that William was not his son, but his wife's illegitimate son from a relationship before they married. He explained that he and his wife were now living apart and she was with another man. He said that if this meant he was legally responsible for William he would do his best for the boy but he was currently in poor circumstances and had to support an aged and invalid mother and

49

had no-one to look after the boy. The Guardians wrote back to say that given the man's circumstances, they would allow William to stay in the Homes for a further two weeks on the condition that his stepfather removed William after this time and pay four shillings for each week that William had been in the Homes. On the 12th February, William's stepfather paid the bill to the Guardians and collected William and he moved in with his stepfather and step grandmother.

BARUM WORKHOUSE
1912: A love story

Sydney was taken to court by the Guardians of the Poor for absconding from the Workhouse and the theft of the suit of Workhouse clothes which he was wearing.

Frederick Watts appeared at the trial and said that Sydney, from Lynton, was an able-bodied man with no reason why he could not earn a living but had been in the Workhouse for around two years. He had been working in the institution's gardens but was erratic and had become increasingly troublesome and, as a result, his leave had been cancelled. In court, Sydney responded to this by saying he had been invalided into the workhouse but, even so, he had "worked like an old horse".

The trial heard that he had fallen in love with a woman called Mary Jane. The Master of the Workhouse told how Sydney had taken to "wasting his time watching Mary Ann through the window". She then left the Workhouse. Desperate to see Mary Ann, and his leave cancelled, he had fled at the first opportunity. For absconding and stealing the clothes, he was sentenced to a month's hard labour in prison.

A few years later, he was a resident of the Devon Mental Hospital in Exmouth. Mary Jane was there at the same time. It was a large hospital with hundreds of patients so they may not have known each other were there. But perhaps they did?

On occasion, the Guardians got involved in a bit of detective work to find out who was financially responsible for the children. For example, one mother was occasionally writing letters to her two illegitimate children who were in the Homes. The Master noticed that on the latest letter, the mother was using a different surname. He gave this information to the Guardians and, at their next meeting, they charged the clerk with the job of seeing what he could find out about her possible change of circumstances. The clerk discovered that she had indeed got married and so the Guardians wrote to her take her children home: it was now her new husband's job to be responsible for the two children. Such was the shame of having illegitimate children that women did not always tell their new husband about them. When the children arrived from the Homes complete with a bill for past maintenance from the Guardians, not all marriages would have survived.

A significant proportion of the time in Guardians' meetings was spent reading letters from other Unions to say that a person from Barnstaple was living in their Union workhouse and so the Guardians needed to pay for their relief. The Barnstaple Guardians were also in contact with, and receiving money from, other Unions for people not from Barnstaple who were in the Barnstaple Workhouse or Homes.

Boarding out

The Barnstaple Guardians of the Poor tried to board out some children with local families. As a forerunner of modern fostering, this entailed finding the child a local family to live with. The children remained the ultimate responsibility of the Guardians.

In the early years of the Homes, there were minimal checks done of the receiving family, particularly if they were related to the child. However, the Guardians later visited the families to ensure that they were suitable, a task generally given to the female Guardians.

Some boarding out arrangements were made when the family proactively approached the Guardians asking if there were suitable children they could take. The Local Government Board in the early years were keen that Barnstaple Guardians only boarded out children who were orphaned or deserted ie. they had no known parents, but this was relaxed over time.

The host families were paid a weekly amount as a contribution to the costs of raising the child. In the early years of the Homes, the Guardians set this amount themselves and were keen to keep it below the weekly cost of keeping the child in the Homes. They regularly got into negotiations with the host families about the rates the Board were willing to pay.

Later, the weekly amount was set by the Government (five shillings a week in 1916) and the Guardians were given a responsibility to visit the children regularly to ensure that all was well.

Older children might be found situations. This differed from boarding out as the children would be working. For example a family with a farm might take on a child from the Homes to have him working in the stables or a business might take a live-in apprentice. The child would be earning money and so could pay for his or her own board so the Guardians generally did not contribute any outrelief. Apart from an initial check, the Guardians would not have anything to do with this relationship once the child was 16. However the host employer could return the child if he were not happy with his work.

In 1904, 14 year old Edward, having finished his education, was sent to Mr C of Stoke Rivers for a month's trial. The Guardians stipulated that "in the event that he [Edward] did not give satisfaction" and was returned to them, he would not be allowed to go back into the Homes but would have to go into the workhouse.

Not all situations turned out to be good for the young person:

————————❖————————

Edith's story

Edith had been placed under the care of the Guardians until she reached the age of 18. As a young girl, the Guardians boarded her out with a couple in Swimbridge, Mr and Mrs M. When she was brought to the Barnstaple Fair with her master one day, she took the opportunity to run off to her parents' house. Edith said that Mrs M had thrashed her with a stick because she was doing work for Mr M and not her, and she had been hit three times before. Two of the Guardians went to meet Mrs M and she denied hitting Edith with a stick but did admit to boxing her ears. Edith was taken from her parents and placed back in the Homes where the Guardians resolved to find her another situation.

In some placements, the child grew attached to the family with whom they were boarded. Archie was boarded out to his host family for eleven years. but, when he was old enough, he was sent to a situation some distance away. Distraught at leaving the host family, particularly the mother, he ran away several times, each time going back to the host family he had left. The Guardians arranged a new situation for him that was near to his old host family, and they agreed to him going back to live with them. He was reportedly very happy to be back with his surrogate mother.

Some boarding out placements lasted for the entirely of the child's childhood. Others went very wrong:

————————❖————————

Dorothy's Story

When Dorothy's parents died suddenly, she and her three younger siblings were placed by the Guardians with Miss R. The Guardians were very happy to have found someone who would take all four of the children.

However, after some time, six year old Dorothy told someone at school that Miss R had thrown pepper into her mouth.

The four children were removed from Miss R's care. Guardians, an Inspector and other officers went to see Miss R who said that it was an accident the pepper got into her mouth. She was only threatening Dorothy with it "when the child caught her arm and knocked the pepper into her own mouth". The Guardians discussed the matter at some length and decided "considering all the circumstances, it was thought that although Miss R was most unwise in her method of punishment, the affair had been a little exaggerated."

One of the officers added however, that on their visit to the family, at 8.30 in the morning Miss R was not downstairs with the children. The children had had no breakfast and had to get to school which was a mile and half away. It was impossible that they could eat and get to school on time.

For this reason the children were found new places to live.

Taking children home

Some parents and other relatives did apply for their children to be returned to them. The practice was that the parent would contact the Guardians by letter telling them of their circumstances and income and their wish to have the child back with them. The Guardians then considered the request at their meeting, and made a decision. In later years, one or more of the Guardians (generally the female Guardians) would be sent to see if the place appeared suitable for the child.

Those children who had been adopted by the Guardians for the entirely of their childhoods because, for example, of abuse or neglect by their parents, were unlikely to have ever been returned to those same parents.

Sometimes, the Guardians' decision on this came down to relatively minor issues. Paying the maintenance bill, for example, or sending an outfit for the child to wear as they could not take their workhouse clothes with them.

BARUM WORKHOUSE
Breaking stones

People in the Workhouse were arguably imprisoned there as if they had committed a crime when most were guilty only of being unable to work. However, those considered to be vagrants, people who travelled and requested poor relief when they could find nowhere to sleep, received a far worse punishment than imprisonment alone. They were forced to break stones during their time at Barnstaple Workhouse. In 1902, a tramp called George was charged with refusing to break stones. Frederick Watts said that George started breaking the stones but soon threw down his hammer and said that he would "sooner go to Exeter". Exeter Prison was indeed where he was sent, for 14 days' imprisonment with hard labour, quite probably breaking more stones.

The Barnstaple Guardians bought in large pieces of limestone for the vagrants to break up. However, in 1904, Frederick Watts reported to the Guardians that the yard was now so full of broken stone, it could not be used. The Guardians struck a deal with Barnstaple Rural District Council who agreed to buy the pieces of stone but at a cost which was less than the stone had cost to buy. The vagrants were allowed to be idol for a time until a cheaper source of stone to be broken could be found.

Mrs F had three children in the Homes and wrote to the Board of Guardians asking if she could have the oldest child returned to her. The Guardians considered her case and agreed as long as Mrs F provided a suitable outfit for the girl. The girl became a domestic servant in Ilfracombe.

In many cases, however it was not down to the parents asking for children to be returned, the Guardians insisted on it:

———————❖———————

George and Lily

In 1907, the Guardians wrote to Mrs M to say that she must take her two children from the Homes now that she was married. She sent a letter back to say that as she only had one bedroom and that she was ill she couldn't take them at this time. Instead she would try to contribute to their maintenance although her husband was only a labourer and their income was 11/- a week, 2/6 of which went on rent.

The Guardians considered her letter at their next meeting and wrote a letter back to her saying that she had to take her children regardless, or they would take appropriate action.

Four months later, during which time, Mrs M's husband had been prosecuted for his failure to take the children, Mrs M wrote again to the Guardians saying that "she did not wish any further proceedings to be taken by the Guardians against her husband as the last fine was a heavy one." She asked the Guardians to return her children to her. The Guardians put George and Lily on the arranged train and asked the Guard to keep an eye on them. They were met at the end of their journey by their mother.

It was not unusual for children to be taken in by more distant relatives when their parents were not able to look after them. The Guardians would always entertain applications from relatives. They asked that they could provide the children with somewhere to live and had enough money to meet the child's basic needs. The Guardians could also make a contribution towards the costs of a child's care in the form of weekly outrelief if they felt there was a need.

———————— ❖ ————————

Victor's Story

Victor, aged ten, was a resident of the Cottage Homes when he was taken one day by his grandmother, who lived in Barnstaple, and she refused to give him back.

The Guardians discussed the matter at their meeting and agreed to inform her that she could not harbour a child who was in the custody of the Guardians. She was given seven days to return Victor and told to pay a fine of £20.

She said she could not afford to pay £20 and she was certainly not going to return her grandchild. She went to the boardroom to meet the Guardians and argue her case.

"I will never send him back!" she said. "I would not return him if you were to kill me." She said they would not "get the poor little fellow back to again punish him." She was escorted out of the boardroom.

One of the Guardians said that Victor's grandmother was "undoubtedly excitable but I respect age" and they discussed whether they could leave the boy with her. However, they decided that her home was not suitable and the Chair said that she was not sending Victor to school and, regardless, they could not go back on a decision already taken.

The Guardians told her that if she did not pay the fine, she would go to prison and Victor would then be sent back to the Cottage Homes anyway. Victor eventually went back to the Homes, There is no record of whether Grandma ever paid the £20 fine.

Leaving the Homes

Some of the children left the Homes early, some going back to live with their own families. Betsy, for example, was born in the workhouse in 1901. When her mother left the House, Betsy went into the Homes. However, within a few years she was back living with her mother, grandmother and sister. Others left as children to go to other institutions such asylums, industrial schools or other institutional homes.

Some children died while in the Cottage Homes. George, for example, was in the Homes alone, no siblings with him and no parent in the workhouse. Tragically he died aged just 11 months old.

By contrast, other children were under the care of the Guardians for their entire childhoods. The children who were in the Cottage Homes were given an education and, in some cases, a situation in which they had a training or experience for their adult working life.

Many of the girls went into domestic service. It was a steady job which was often live-in and so ideal for a young person who had no family to stay with. For boys, going into military service had the same advantages.

Edwin, having spent the entirety of his childhood in the Cottage Homes joined the Navy and saw the world. His sister went to live with an aunt and got a job making hosiery.

Sadly, it did not turn out well for all. Amy, for example, as a young adult was back in an institution. She went to a 'rescue home for fallen women' in Plymouth - a place where women who were thought to be morally insufficient, perhaps having had an illegitimate child, spent their days doing laundry to earn their keep.

The children's Cottage Homes were not always suitable for all the children taken there. But. In the early days, there were few alternative places to send children, particularly those who were ill or had disabilities. While facilities existed in some of the larger towns and cities of England, they were few and far between in our south west corner.

Some children spent their entire childhoods waiting for somewhere more appropriate to live:

––––––––––❖––––––––––

Percy's Story

Percy went into Barnstaple Cottage Homes with his mother, older brother and baby sister.

Although their mother left the workhouse, the children stayed and spent their childhoods in the Cottage Homes.

Percy was found to have epilepsy while he was still in the Homes. When he was twelve it was reported to the Guardians that his fits were getting worse. They decided that he needed to go to a specialist institution. Sadly, there was nowhere local at that time. The Guardians contacted the Meath Home for Epileptics but they said they couldn't take him as they only took girls.

The Guardians then contacted the Lingfield Epileptics Home in Surrey. They replied that they were full but would add him to their waiting list. Two years later, Percy's school, St Mary's, contacted the Guardians to say they could no longer look after Percy because of the frequency and severity of his fits. It was not, however, until the following May that a place was found for him at the Manchester Epileptics Institution. In another set back the new Institution said they would charge the Barnstaple Guardians £70 a year for Percy to stay there. The Guardians decided to delay the decision. The school again said that he could not stay with them. Finally, he given a place in the Lingfield Home. He was then 14 years old.

Tragically, Percy died five years later.

Freddie's Story

When Freddie was seven, despite the headmaster saying they had no room for him, Freddie was taken to the gates of the new Ashleigh Road School where he was turned away by the headmaster. Ultimately, however, they did give him a place there because it was a shorter walk from the Cottage Homes than his previous school and he had difficulties walking.

Freddie was born in Barnstaple Workhouse and left there. When he was four, the Guardians decided to find him a family to live with as the Cottage Homes weren't suitable for him. Unfortunately, they couldn't find him a placement. Over the next twelve years, the Guardians unsuccessfully looked for a more suitable home for Freddie, and approached different institutions asking if Freddie could have a place with them including the NSPCC, reformatories, The Lord Mayor Treloar Cripples' Home in Cheshire, the Waifs & Strays, and the National Children's Home. When he was 16, a local family took him but brought him back just two weeks later.

Two years later, in 1917, having left the workhouse, the Guardians heard (by requests for indoor relief payments) that he was first in Taunton Union Workhouse and then in St Thomas Union Workhouse in Exeter. In 1918, the Guardians of the St Thomas Union again contacted the Barnstaple Guardians asking if they would pay outdoor relief for Freddie as he was now in digs but he was not earning enough to support himself. Two years later, when he was 18, the St Thomas Union Guardians wrote again. This time they said how extremely well-behaved, deserving, industrious and steady Freddie was but that his current outrelief payments were very small. The Barnstaple Board agreed an increase from 3/- per week to 5/- per week.

A few months later, Freddie was in hospital in London. The Barnstaple Guardians stopped his outdoor relief payments as they had no financial liability for him while he was in a hospital. At Westminster Hospital, he was seen by eminent surgeon Sir James Stewart who said he must have his right leg amputated below the knee to get relief from his "present grave lameness".

The Barnstaple Guardians received a letter from the surgeon asking for financial support for Freddie from the Union. The Barnstaple Guardians wrote back to say that they could not pay him any outrelief but if he "required any little extras in the hospital such as tea, sugar etc. they would be prepared to assist". Sir James operated on Freddie and amputated one of his legs.

When Freddie left the hospital and returned to Exeter, the St Thomas Union Relieving Officer and Medical Officer both recommended that he return to Barnstaple Workhouse. The Medical Officer said Freddie was "permanently crippled and in digs which were unsuitable. I considered it not a fit home as there were four others sleeping in the same bedroom. He has been told to rest as much as possible and is always about the streets (having no real home). He has already had a fall and been taken home in an ambulance. He appears to have no friends in Exeter to assist him."

Freddie travelled to Barnstaple to meet with Guardians in the boardroom of the workhouse. He explained he did not want to return to the workhouse but he might need some outdoor relief while he got himself settled. He found digs back in Exeter in a coffee tavern and got work as a boot maker.

In 1922, when Freddie was in his early twenties, he was back in the newspapers. It was reported that he was travelling from place to place, asking for help and leaving when the goodwill ran out. He had travelled by train from Hull to Nottingham where he was arrested for not paying the fare. Freddie was told that "we don't want such men as you in Nottingham. You must go back to Hull." Fortunately, the rail company withdrew the charge and the magistrates agreed to make him a grant of 12/- from the poor box to pay his fare back to Hull.

- I have been able to find no further trace of Freddie.

Complaints & illegitimacy

The 1920s began with a clear indication that not all was well for the children in the Homes. The Local Government Board had been replaced by the Ministry of Health but the annual inspections continued. At this time, they had raised no problems. For example the 1920 report was largely good:

"Institution in very good condition. Inmates appeared as comfortable under the new master and matron as they were under the late officers. With regard to weak-minded children, I find the Guardians doing what they can, still, they should now endeavour to get the county council to take some of the weak-minded children."

However, a very different view of the suitability of the Homes had developed locally. In 1920, local newspapers were covering serious incidents involving boys running away. Two boys were found guilty of stealing a bottle of mineral water while absconding from the Homes. They were sentenced to six strokes of the birch. Absconding was certainly not uncommon at this time:

———————❖———————

James F's Story

James went into the Cottage Homes in 1918 with his sisters. James was six, his older sister was nine and his little sister was just three. Their parents had both died and there was nowhere else for the children to go. In 1920, when he had just turned nine, James was in the yard of the boys' cottage when he climbed the wall and ran off. He spent a day in Barnstaple and went playing by the cricket field. He came back to the cottage where he was seen by his Foster Mother climbing back into the yard over the wall.

She found money in his pocket and, when she heard that a wallet had been stolen in the town, she searched and found the (now empty) wallet hidden behind the wall of the yard James was charged with theft and the case went before the magistrates. At the trial, Frank George, the Master, testified that although he was intelligent, James was also an accomplished thief and had stolen from the Foster Mother before. James cried throughout the case. He was sent, for his crime, to Exeter Industrial School until he was 16, a seven year sentence. These were notoriously harsh places of strict discipline and hard work. Leaving his sisters behind in the Homes, James was now on his own.

As a result of incidents of absconding from the Homes coupled with absenteeism from school, the clerk to the Education Committee chose to write to the Guardians on more than one occasion with a warning that if there were not 'drastic alterations' to what he perceived as poor conditions and discipline for the children in the Homes, he would ensure that the matter was brought before the Education Committee and attendance orders applied for.

In addition to the letters, there was talk in the town about the treatment of the children and the conditions in the Homes. Some of the boys were reported as having made complaints of bad treatments in the Homes.

The Guardians discussed the issues at length. On some points they were in agreement. For example, the clerk to the Education Committee complained that a girl he described as an 'imbecile'[5] was staying in the Homes which he said was both unacceptable and illegal. He also criticised the facilities available in the Homes. The Guardians accepted both points. They said they had been trying to find more appropriate accommodation for the girl for some time. Because the only current alternative was the workhouse which they did not feel was suitable for her, the Inspector of the Ministry of Health had given permission for the girl to stay in the Cottage Homes. The Guardians also pointed out that the boys could have chosen to behave and had to take some responsibility for their actions.

---------❖---------

John and Ernest's story

John was eight and his little brother Ernest was six when their father died of consumption (tuberculosis). Since then, their mother had been receiving five shillings per week for the three of them. She paid two shillings in rent for her cottage which, when the matter was discussed in court was agreed left her with only a meagre amount to live on. The court felt that getting a job was not within her capabilities. For a few years, the NSPCC had been involved with the family and had given her warnings about her care of the boys. However, in 1920, the court heard that things were in a very bad way. They were not badly nourished but the house was in a awful state and was described in court as verminous. She argued that she did her best to keep everything clean and look after her sons. The court found, despite general agreement that "she was not in a good mental condition", she was guilty of neglect of her sons. She was sentenced to a month in prison. The Guardians adopted the boys until the age of 18 and they went to live in the Cottage Homes. They would not live with their mother again as children.

They were, however, at a loss as to what to do about discipline. The two boys who were the main culprits had been split up, one being sent to live in the House – "in an effort to separate the sheep from the goats," the Chair, William T Buckingham joked. After the laughter, he went on to say that the workhouse was not a proper place for boys to be in and some day the Board would have to change this. The Guardians discussed whether appointing a man to work in the Homes would help with discipline.

On the matter of play facilities for the children, the Guardians agreed that these were not sufficient. What the boys wanted, the meeting felt, was a proper place to go outside school hours. Currently, they were coming home from school, having their dinner and were told to go into the 'little yard' behind the boys' home. The yard of cottage 1 (in which boys were generally placed) was particularly small, half the size of the other yards. Left to their devices in this small space, the boys were bored, climbed the wall, and ran away. There was "no place in which they could play or do anything", another Guardian agreed. "It was horrible to be cooped up as they were at present", said another.

The House Committee had met the day before to discuss the matter and had made suggestions, including appointing a married couple to manage the children in the Homes. The Guardians also considered making the flower beds at the front of the

Boys playing in rock park c1912

house into a play area, or appointing a man to escort them to the local park.

However, no immediate decisions were made other than to hope that things would improve for the boys when the weather got better. The matter was referred back to the House Committee who appointed a sub-committee to examine the idea of selling the Cottage Homes so that more suitable accommodation could be bought.

The following autumn, the matter came back to the Guardians' meeting for their consideration.

The meeting began with the revelation that, of the £2,200 the Union had borrowed to fund the building of the Cottage Homes, nearly £890 remained to be paid back, a factor which may have determined how much they might have been able to raise for relocating. The Union had repaid an average of less than £70 a year.

———————❖———————

Olive's story

Olive was eight years old. Her father had died two years earlier having taken his own life having spent some time without work. Her mother was now dying of cancer in Ilfracombe. Olive and her younger brother, aged seven, had no family locally other than their mother. Distraught at what might happen to her children. Olive's mother made plans as best she could. She sent her son to live with an uncle in Northumberland.

On her behalf, the NSPCC contacted the Guardians of the Poor to ask if Olive could be sent to an industrial school in the south of England as her uncle lived nearby and she might be able to visit him in the holidays. The Guardians, receiving her letter tried to dissuade her as industrial schools were harsh places for children who were thought to be criminals, and no holidays were given. They explained that the very act of being in an industrial school "might be prejudicial to her in later life" such was the shame of being sent there. They said it would be much better for Olive if she would go to the Cottage Homes. However, Olive's mother could not be persuaded and Olive was sent away. A matter of weeks later, Olive's mother died.

At this meeting, although the indiscipline of the early summer was mentioned as the reason behind these considerations, the idea of the play area for the children was not brought up. Instead, the meeting focused on having somewhere to grow produce which could be used in the workhouse and Cottage Homes. The idea of selling the current buildings and moving to the country was raised but the meeting voted against largely on the grounds of the cost. Instead the meeting agreed to look for a garden or allotment which they could rent in the town.

The idea of relocating the Homes never really went away, however. A few years later, the Board of Guardians were considering buying Ashleigh House and grounds to give the children more space and, specifically, more outside space. Again, it was decided it was too expensive an outlay.

Borrowing the entire cost of the building of the Cottage Homes in 1901 was a decision made on a good premise. The ratepayers, a group which included the Guardians themselves, would not have liked a sudden hike in their annual bill. However, after 20 years, only 60% of the loan had been repaid even though wages and property values has risen and interest had not been charged.

It could be argued that this slow rate of repayment, putting as little pressure on the ratepayers as possible, was acting as a barrier to change. While the Guardians' meetings regularly discussed and agreed that the children needed more outside space, the cost of making any significant changes on top of the loan repayments always brought the discussions to an end without any resolution.

BARUM WORKHOUSE
1923: Stealing a suit

William wanted to leave the Workhouse and so simply walked out of the door one day. No-one stopped him so he thought he was free. However, he found himself arrested and then in court charged with stealing. When he walked out he only had his workhouse uniform. The Doctor testified that William had not intended to cause any harm but he had no clothes of his own. He was cautioned and sent back to the workhouse, in his workhouse clothes.

Workhouse nursery

The Cottage Homes were built to take children out of the workhouse which as they would mix with people who were a bad influence and the taint of the place would hold them back in adulthood. This was the view in the late nineteenth century and the Local Government Board pushed for significant investment by the Poor Law Unions throughout the country to achieve this. However, the Barnstaple Union, despite their efforts and the establishment of the Cottage Homes, did not manage to keep children out of the workhouse.

Various reports to the Guardians revealed that there were times when there were more children than could be accommodated in the Homes. The initial maximum was set at fifteen children per cottage. There were times when this increased by just one or two but also times when there was no room in the Homes for all the children. At the time of the 1911 census there were 57 children most of whom were in the Homes but some had to live in the workhouse.

Soon afterwards, this arrangement was formalised with the creation of a nursery in the workhouse itself. At the time of the 1921 census, there were 41 children in the Homes but a further ten in the workhouse

Of the ten children living in the workhouse, Sidney was the youngest, being just twelve days old, Olive was four months and there were eight other children who

The offices in Castle Street from where the clerk to the Board of Guardians operated.

were aged between a year old and 5½ years old. Sidney was an illegitimate child who had been born in the workhouse, probably because his mother could not work while pregnant.

Mary Ann's mother was recorded as having died, Mary Ann now being three years old. All the other children in the workhouse were recorded as being illegitimate although, like Mary Ann, Pamela's mother had died. The children were in the workhouse alone, without any relatives.

The House was a place primarily of elderly people with 50 of the 106 adults living there being aged 60 or older - the oldest being 90 years old. The average life expectancy was only a little over 50 years old at that time in England.

Having the nursery in the workhouse was not ideal, although staff were appointed to look after them. It suggests that perhaps a nursery really needed to have been added in the Homes when they were first built. Adding one retrospectively was beyond what the Guardians wanted to spend. However, the nursery remained in the workhouse for the next 25 years.

—————❖—————

Harry's story

Harry was two and half years old, an illegitimate baby. His mother, going out to work, left him with a friend and paid her £1 a month to take care of him. Neighbours tried to get food to the boy who they said was alone and crying every day. They grew so worried about Harry that they contacted the NSPCC who found him in a terrible state - emaciated, filthy, infected with lice and suffering from rickets. The woman who was looking after him herself went to work as a charwoman from 9 o'clock in the morning until 9 o'clock in the evening every day. In court, she said that she came home to see him at dinner time although neighbours said that this was only when she had washing to hang out. She also said that she left her own little boy, Ronnie, to look after him but admitted that he often left him to go and play.

The court ordered that Harry be taken into the workhouse and that the woman charged with caring for him should be sent to prison for a month with hard labour. This left Ronnie needing someone to care for him too.

A legitimate issue

The census of 1921 was the first to record the legitimacy of the children of the Barnstaple Workhouse and Cottage Homes. For each child, it was recorded whether their parents were alive or dead and whether they were illegitimate. From the discussion recorded at the meetings of the Guardians, we know that the children in the workhouse and Cottage Homes were often born outside of marriage and that this, in itself, was a factor in them coming into the care of the Guardians of the Poor. Without a husband, the mothers of illegitimate babies were often shunned by friends, neighbours and potential employers as there was a sense of shame put on the shoulders of the women. While the men were able to continue on with their lives a woman, with a baby to look after, could find life very difficult indeed.

The reason for recording the illegitimacy of the residents of the Cottage Homes may have been to look at the impact of the upheaval of the Great War on family structure. It may also have given an indication of the financial liability of the Unions as illegitimate fathers had no financial liability unless their paternity could be proven in some way, not easy task until DNA testing in the late twentieth century.

Of the 51 children in the workhouse and the Cottage Homes in 1921, 29 were recorded as being illegitimate. For a further eight children, their parents were not known and so it was impossible to say whether they were legitimate or not. This means that around two-thirds of the children in the Homes were illegitimate in

---

BARUM WORKHOUSE
1924: a great age

1924 saw the birthday of the oldest inmate of the workhouse. Mrs T was 101 in August and she received congratulations from the King, George V. The Guardians put on a birthday tea for her. She had lived independently in Barnstaple until she reached the age of one hundred when she went into the Workhouse.

comparison with just 7.5% of births in England generally being illegitimate at that time. Now, around half of births are outside marriage with, both legally and socially, greatly reduced significance on either the child or the parent

In the times of the Poor Laws, illegitimate children were still referred to as 'bastards', their mothers' as 'loose' or 'fallen' women and even the chances of survival of babies born out of marriage were questioned. In 1908, a Royal Commission on the Poor Law requested from the Guardians "statistics showing what effect the fact of illegitimacy might have upon the chance of survival of babies born in the workhouse."

◆

Public Appointments

Barnstaple Union

APPOINTMENT OF A FOSTER MOTHER

The Guardians of the above Union invite APPLICATIONS from suitable persons, preferably those with experience, for the post of FOSTER MOTHER at one of their Cottage Homes on Alexandra_road, Barnstaple. The salary will be £40 per annum with the usual allowances for Board and Washing & c., and subject to deductions for Health and Pensions Insurance. No persons over 42 years of age need apply.

Applications in Forms to be obtained from me to be returned to me no later than Friday Noon, 15th February 1929.

By the Order of the Board. Martin Sykes, Clerk
23 Castle Street, Barnstaple
1st February 1929

◆

The Guardians changed their adverts during this time to include a stipulation that women applying to be foster mothers should be no older than 42.

Treats for the children

Throughout the lifetime of the Homes, local people and businesses gave the children treats. These included a wide range of items for which presumably the children had a range of enthusiasm. For example, gifts of flowers to decorate the houses may have been less popular than gifts of sweets which were also donated at times.

The 1920s, with deepening post-war economic depression, were a difficult time for many people, including those in Barnstaple but still the children of the Homes were not forgotten. On Christmas day, Charles Darbyshire, The Grand Old Man of Ilfracombe, gave the men of the workhouse tobacco, sweets for the children and tea for the women. Gertrude George, the Matron, donated a Christmas tree for the nursery in the workhouse. Two of the Guardians made cakes for the Homes. The owner of the Barnstaple Picturedrome gave all the children free tickets.

In the summer, Charles Darbyshire took all the children of the Homes and workhouse to Instow for the day for their annual holiday. They left Barnstaple at 8am and played sports and games on the beach. A tea was given to them in the Black Horse and they all got back to Barnstaple by 10pm.

The children were also given fireworks for Bonfire night, and there was once an unbelievable donation of 800 eggs from the congregation of the Combe Martin Baptist Church.

BARUM WORKHOUSE
1925: dirty washing

At a meeting of the Guardians, the matter of the laundry facilities was raised. Only one person had applied to the vacant post of laundry woman. Somebody needs to warn her, one of the Guardians said, that the facilities are 'prehistoric'. Another, more seriously, asked how long the workhouse could continue in this slipshod way. "The time was long overdue for changing the hand laundry to one of power. It was a treadmill business that they were up against all the time and they could not find a penal establishment anywhere whose work was done under similar conditions". Washing clothes and bedding for 160 people without the benefit of electricity certainly seems like a tall order for one person.

ILFRACOMBE'S GRAND OLD MAN

There were many people, mostly men, who successfully stood for election as members of Barnstaple's Guardians of the Poor. Some served for decades, others for only a year or two. Some drove the work of the Board, others were less active. One, however, was unmatched in his personal generosity to the people in the institutions. He was Charles Darbyshire JP.

Despite being born in Lancashire and having an early career in Argentina (where he met his wife Eliza), he made Ilfracombe his home and he took a keen interest in all levels of local activity. He held many public roles in North Devon, including president of Ilfracombe Lifeboat service and many trade and civic organisations. He had a habit of giving gifts and parties for the school children of the town. Such was his enthusiasm and generosity that he was known as Ilfracombe's Grand Old Man.

Charles was a very keen walker. He walked at least nine miles every day, and did so into his late eighties. "My rule of life," he once said. "Is only two meals a day, and these are not large ones."

Charles was on the Barnstaple Board of Guardians from at least 1882 until his death in 1929. During this time he took the children of the Workhouse, and then of the Cottage Homes, together with some of the women of the Workhouse, on annual trips, often to Ilfracombe. They were taken in groups in charabancs (pictured below). For decades, he made weekly gifts to the children, strawberries or other fruit, buns or money. One of his last philanthropic acts before he died, aged 94, was to give every person in the workhouse and every child in the Cottage Homes a Christmas card.

The end of the Poor Law

In 1930, there were huge changes for the Poor Law and the workhouses that had dominated provision for poor people throughout the previous century. The Local Government Act of 1929 shifted the responsibility for provision for poor people away from Poor Law Unions and their Guardians to local authorities. The legislation was intended to abolish Poor Law Unions, the Poor Law Guardians and the workhouses. The country's cottage homes though, largely remained.

In practice, however, the transition from Poor Laws to local authorities took some time and this was evident in Barnstaple. With more than a hundred mostly elderly or infirm people plus children still resident in Barnstaple Workhouse, it was decided that change had to be gradual and the workhouse role was largely maintained with the Master and Matron still running it. However, the word 'workhouse' was removed and it instead became the Public Assistance Institution. Amongst locals, however, the workhouse name took longer to fade.

A county-wide Public Assistance Committee took on overall responsibility for the Public Assistance Institution and the children's Cottage Homes in Barnstaple along with all those in the rest of Devon. The Committee was based in Exeter.

However, the Barnstaple Guardians of the Poor did not disappear. They continued to hold their fortnightly meetings to discuss the day to day running of the Institution and the Homes although they operated under the county's Public

---

BARUM WORKHOUSE
1931: A suicide

A tragic event took place in Swimbridge when a man was found in Kerscott Woods. William, a 60 year old musician from Ilfracombe had hanged himself from a tree using strips of sacking knotted together. He was found in the evening and cut down but, by that time, he had already died.

An inquest found that he had committed suicide having absconded, without anyone knowing, from Barnstaple Workhouse earlier that same day. He had gone into the Workhouse in 1925 and had spent the last six years living there.

BARUM WORKHOUSE
Joey and Jimmy

The workhouse at Barnstaple had long had a four-legged resident. Used for carrying goods into the workhouse and wood out of the workhouse was a donkey who lived on site and was looked after by one of the inmates. Joey served in the House from 1912 but, when he started refusing to eat anything but sugar in April 1935, the vet was called. He prescribed a fortnight's rest which Joey spent as a guest of Rosalie Chichester at Arlington Court. She felt he would enjoy the company of her own donkey and ponies. He did enjoy his break but it didn't cure him. Rosalie suggested firmly that he should stay at Arlington to enjoy retirement. The Guardians agreed to this although were also keen to put on record that he would be very seriously missed as the inmates loved talking to him and petting him.

The Public Assistance Committee in Exeter felt that Joey's job could be taken by an inmate with a handcart but the Guardians disagreed and immediately advertised for another donkey. Jimmy came from the Railway Hotel in Lympstone, was six years old. Two years after he arrived, the Guardians' meeting was taken up with news that Jimmy had got out, chasing a dog. While out, he managed to cause some expensive damage including dents to the Relieving Officer's car. Despite this, the Chair declared "I am glad we have got such a lively donkey!"

Jimmy's escape was covered in the local papers: he was quite a celebrity; a familiar sight in the town and a friend to many of the inmates in the House.

Assistance Committee and their decision-taking powers were increasingly transferred to Exeter.

The declining financial situation in Britain from the mid 1920s paved the way for the Depression of the early 1930s. Unemployment was generally high, wages were low. Housing was poor, working conditions for many were poor and strikes and unrest were rife. The newly-formed Public Assistance Committee in Exeter were feeling the pressure of high levels of need and rising costs. To add to these pressures, news of critical Ministry of Heath inspection reports of the Barnstaple Cottage Homes made damning headlines in the local newspapers of 1931:

Exeter and Plymouth Gazette
DAILY TELEGRAM.

"NOT SUITABLE"
Barnstaple Cottage Homes criticised

North Devon Journal
For Barnstaple, Bideford, Torrington, Southmolton, Ilfracombe, and other parts of the North of Devon:

BARNSTAPLE COTTAGE HOMES AGAIN
Health Inspectors' Extraordinary Report

The North Devon Herald
AND GENERAL ADVERTISER FOR DEVONSHIRE, EAST CORNWALL & WEST SOMERSET

Cottage Homes Condemned

Exeter and Plymouth Gazette
DAILY TELEGRAM.

CHILDREN'S HOMES
Accommodation shortage in the County

Poor reports

From the discussions and correspondence with the Public Assistance Committee and the annual inspection reports of the Ministry of Health in 1931 and 1933, we can build up a picture of the issues raised about the buildings themselves:

- The baths and toilets needed replacing and all the bathroom facilities needed updating.

- The houses were in need of redecoration throughout

- The kitchens were of a type which could be found in a typical family home, and thus unsuitable for cooking for so many children.

- Stoves were needed to replace the grates currently used for cooking.

- There were either no outdoor play facilities in the yards behind each cottage or they were so dilapidated that they could not be used. And the yards were really too small for play.

- There were no playrooms indoors.

- The rooms were lofty and well-lit but were not homely. For example, there were no curtains in the downstairs windows which had privacy glass to prevent people looking in, but that also meant that the children could not look out.

At the fortnightly Guardians' meetings in which the Inspection reports were discussed, there was a general consensus that the Homes were in need of repair. Quite why this situation had arisen was not quite so clear cut.

The Guardians argued both that they had deliberately reduced spending because of the desperate financial state of the country and also that they had requested money for repairs from the Public Assistance Committee which had not yet been received. The level of disrepair described suggests that the process of neglect may have begun before the Public Assistance Committee was formed.

These issues of culpability would have been of no interest to the children, of course. Nor to the Foster Mothers who were trying to work in less than ideal conditions. The key issue to them was that the Cottage Homes were in what the Ministry of Health Inspector described as "a deplorable state". Not all Guardians, however, agreed things were that bad. The Guardians agreed that decorating was needed and the sanitaryware had to be replaced, for example, but there was no consensus on other matters. The question of play areas was hotly debated. Some felt that a play area was essential, others thought that the Foster Mothers could take children to the public park instead.

One Guardian considered that the "present conditions were dangerous to the health of the children". At the other end of the spectrum, another considered that the Homes were suitable just as they were. Looking at the bigger picture, some simply felt that it was right to be focusing on saving money rather than spending it while the country's economic situation was so bad.

The Ministry of Health inspectors not only found fault with the buildings but also raised other concerns. The reports repeatedly stated that each child should have their own locker in which to keep personal items; that children should be in local boy scouts and girl guides groups and that, the 'low class' neighbours meant that the children could hear bad language. It was the Inspector's opinion that the Homes should be relocated to the countryside.

From the tone of the meetings, it seems that the Guardians did not always take the criticism well. Although they accepted some of the issues with the Homes, they found the suggestion of lockers "ridiculous" and sarcastically expressed their relief that there was never any bad language to be heard in the countryside.

The formation of the Public Assistance Committee in Exeter, and the consequent reduction of the autonomy and power of the Guardians was all very new, having only been put in place in 1930. It seems that the relationship between the two

BARUM WORKHOUSE
1932: coming into money

In March 1932, an inmate of the workhouse, 65 year old John James, unexpectedly received £1,000 in unpaid wages from a job he had had thirty years earlier. His employer at that time had been in such debt that he couldn't pay him but repaid his employee as soon as he could – which turned out to be three decades later.

John James hadn't worked for some time as he was a coachman and the new popularity of the car meant that his skills in driving horse drawn vehicles were no longer required. He decided to enjoy himself when he received his unexpected windfall. Firstly though, he paid £425 to the Guardians of the Poor for his stay in the workhouse and he then gave £300 to his wife and his son who were living in London. Debts paid, he spent the rest visiting friends in Paris. By August, it was reported, having spent all the money, he was back in a workhouse, this time in Liverpool.

bodies had not fully gelled. One local newspaper headline declared the Guardians felt they were "treated like a lot of children" by their new bosses in Exeter.

The Guardians became frustrated when they asked for money for repairs and improvements from the Public Assistance Committee and the response was a request that the Guardians look for suitable premises in the countryside. While they could see that there was no point investing money in buildings which could soon be replaced, it left the Homes in disrepair.

There were also concerns that there was seemingly no plan about the type and extent of the replacement accommodation which would be needed. There was uncertainty about whether the new building was for Barnstaple children or for the whole county and concerns about how education could be provided by small village schools for a large number of Cottage Homes children. The months of discussion on the subject stretched into years and while efforts were made to find alternative accommodation, none could be agreed upon.

The essential repairs and maintenance issues, however, were carried out which must have been a relief for the Foster Mothers who were having to deal with the conditions and must have improved life for the children.

Throughout this time, there remained between 40 and 50 children in the Cottage Homes with roughly around 15 children still living in the Public Assistance Institution at any one time. While the Cottage Homes buildings had their critics as old-fashioned and unsuitable for residential childcare, the former workhouse buildings were now a century old.

Since the end of the workhouse, the average age of the residents in the institution had steadily increased as had the proportion who were there because it was considered that they had mental illness or perhaps a learning disability. While the workhouse had initially been a place where people worked, it was now a place where most of the residents were not able to work. More and more, the provision was about care rather than discipline and work.

The Cottage Homes children still visited the old workhouse building as the boardroom remained the venue for special teas and afternoons of entertainment.

Throughout the time of the Homes, summer trips had generally been a single day by the sea where children enjoyed sports and games on the beach and a tea laid on by a local group or the Guardians. In the summer of 1938, the children went to Instow for a day courtesy of the Devon Constabulary but also 22 children from the Homes were sent to the South Molton children's home for a fortnight's holiday. The events of the next few years, however, meant that this did not happen again for them.

Conduct money

In 1936, the Guardians started giving the children weekly conduct money. This was pocket money given to the children if they had behaved themselves. The amounts ranged from a penny for those aged five to four pence (4d.) for the oldest children. The children wrote letters to the Guardians thanking them for the scheme.

Some quotes from the letters:

"Each week I shall put some of it in the bank, and the rest I shall save for treats, or for if there is a good picture in Barnstaple with Gracie Fields or Shirley Temple."

"If I go anywhere I will now be able to pay for myself like other children."

"I hope when I am grown up I shall also be kind and think of others."

"I feel as if I am grown up, and shall be able to call Saturdays my pay day."

"I am glad we have something to look forward to."

What did the conduct money buy? The answer is that in 1936, there was very little that any but the oldest children could have bought with their weekly pennies without saving up. A packet of a new product called Maltesers cost around 2d. Another new product was a Rowntree's chocolate covered wafer bar. It was named KitKat in 1937 and would have cost the children 2d. A bottle of Coca Cola was priced 6d. Packets of crisps were yet to be mass-produced as it was to be another decade before Golden Wonder and Walkers were widely available.

A cinema ticket would have been around 3d. while a copy of the Beano was a bargain at 2d. Requiring some serious saving, Dr Seuss had just had his first children's book published. A copy would have set the children back more than three shillings!

The impact of war

The year of 1939 saw a spike of flu cases in various parts of England, a not unusual occurrence until the annual flu vaccination programme was introduced in the 1960s. The Homes also experienced an outbreak. Although several lives were claimed in the Public Assistance Institution and there were some staffing issues as officers became ill, the Homes managed to contain the flu and the children recovered.

Only a short time afterwards thoughts were turning to a much less containable problem, a second world war. The Barnstaple Area Guardians Committee (the new name for the Guardians of the Poor) got busy looking at the Air Raid Precautions for the Public Assistance Institution and the Cottage Homes. Blackout was a key issue as there were no curtains downstairs in the Homes and there were many windows in the former workhouse buildings. In case of severe supply problems, the Guardians planned to make use of wells in the institution's grounds. They ordered a petrol pump so that the water could be brought up to the surface. Very shortly after these plans were put in place, war was declared.

The aim of the Guardians was to keep things running as near as possible to normal for the sake of those in the Public Assistance Institution and in the Homes. However, change was inevitable at such a time.

Food was rationed in Britain from 1940. Ration books were issued which detailed exactly what could be bought. Initially, food such as bacon, ham, butter, and sugar could only be purchased with limited ration coupons and then other items like meat, cheese, margarine, eggs, milk, tea, breakfast cereals, rice, and biscuits were restricted. Dried milk (left) and powdered eggs became the norm. Clothing, fuel, and soap were also rationed. Rationing was not fully lifted until the 1950s.

One early change impacted on the Guardians as a committee although, arguably, not so much on the children. For 105 years, the Guardians had attended a meeting every fortnight in the workhouse building. Every other Friday afternoon since 1834, twenty to thirty of the Guardians met for two hours to discuss all the matters of concern to them. The county's Public Assistance Committee, however, said that economy must come first and that meetings should now be held only once every two months.

Already feeling sidelined in the management of their own institutions by their new bosses, having their meeting time cut was a cause of consternation amongst the Guardians. It was a very tangible indicator of their reduced powers. After significant discussion, the Guardians reluctantly agreed to meet just once a month.

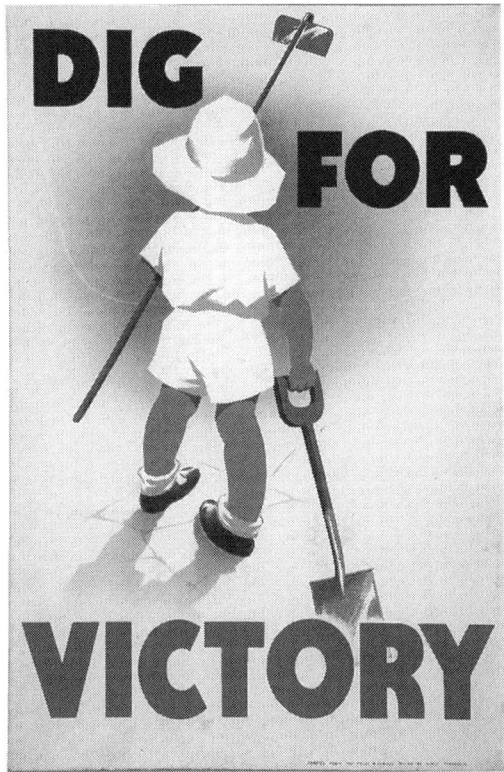

During the war years, the Guardians had to concern themselves with the domestic consequences of the fighting. Providing food and the other things needed for the residents of the Homes and the Public Assistance Institution was a very significant problem. Some items simply were no longer available, others shot up in price because of their scarcity.

Some children's Cottage Homes, such as Manston Cottage Homes in Ramsgate had land which could be used for growing crops and raising livestock for meat and milk supplies. Even the city-based homes, Erdington Cottage Homes in north Birmingham, for example, had gardens and space that they could utilise for growing vegetables. The Birmingham children also raised rabbits to supplement their diet. Barnstaple's Public Assistance Institution, however, had very little land, most of their gardens having been given up - such as those on the site where the Cottage Homes were built. The Homes themselves had only small yards leaving the Guardians almost completely reliant on outside sources of food.

Christmas in wartime

The Guardians were keen to hold Christmas and New Year celebrations for the patients of the Institution and the children of the Homes despite the war. Festivities everywhere, however, were very changed.

Christmas 1941 in North Devon was described as a quiet, stay at home time with only limited travel. Prayers were said for peace in Barnstaple's St Mary's Church and a prominent 'V' featured in the decorations at the Infirmary. For the Public Assistance Institution, beer and minerals were provided for the inmates and the Salvation Army Band and Sydney Harper (a local musician) provided the entertainment as they did at Christmas celebrations in the Institution throughout the war. The children of the Homes were shown a Ministry of Information film on Christmas Eve and were treated to a bit of turkey with their dinner on Christmas Day.

For the Christmas of 1942, after listening to music from the Salvation Army band and Sydney Harper, the children of the Homes put on a play for everyone in the Public Assistance Institution called *The Sleeping Princess*. Local people made dolls for the children and gave tobacco for the men of the Institution.

In 1943 Christmas presents for the children were given by the National Fire Service and cakes were donated by the Air Training Corps. The manager of the Regal Cinema on the Strand (right) gifted free cinema tickets.

---◆---

A story of neglect

In 1941, a Barnstaple woman whose husband was a soldier at war, was prosecuted by the NSPCC for the neglect of her four young children in what was described as a sad and sordid story. The court was told of an instance when her five year old son, unsupervised, went to the coal cellar to fetch coal. It was dark so he took a candle to see by. Unfortunately, his nightshirt caught fire and he came back into the house in flames. He suffered burns which his mother tried to explain away as being caused by an accident with indoor fireworks. As a result of an NSPCC inspector visiting the house, the four children had already been sent to the Cottage Homes. Gertrude George, the Matron, testified that all the children were putting on weight now they were there. The children's mother, when questioned, said she was not guilty of neglect but, as she could not work while looking after her children, "it was a struggle to live" on the money she received. She was sentenced to four months' imprisonment and the children were to stay in the Homes.

BARUM WORKHOUSE
1941: missing clothes

A 52 year old man in the Public Assistance Institution asked the Board of Guardians for a suit of clothes as his own had gone missing. He was a hairdresser by profession and, having posted an advert in a trade paper, he had received more than 30 replies and had found decent work. To take up the job, however, he needed clothes as he only had the Workhouse clothes he had been loaned. Frank George told the Guardians that, before coming to the Public Assistance Institution , he had been living in caves in Berrynarbor and, when he arrived, his clothes were so verminous and filthy that they had been destroyed. On this occasion, the Guardians were happy to provide him with clothes so that he could begin his new life outside.

Evacuation

As war went on, problems of finding staff and retaining them occupied the Guardians as so many local people were involved in the war effort. Another pressing issue was the influx of elderly people into the Institution who were not destitute but simply could not find anyone to look after them. With more elderly residents than working age people, there were fewer able to work.

Barnstaple, not being a place of major military importance, saw little direct action. There was one bomb dropped on the town but fortunately it caused very little damage. However, the War brought other changes. Thousands of American troops arrived in North Devon to train on the coast for the D Day landings. This turned out to be the most significant victory for the Western Allies making the end of the war a real possibility. Here for many months, their presence and their American ways, had a significant impact on life in Barnstaple. Tragically, many of the estimated 14,000 American men who trained in North Devon lost their lives in the D Day mission.

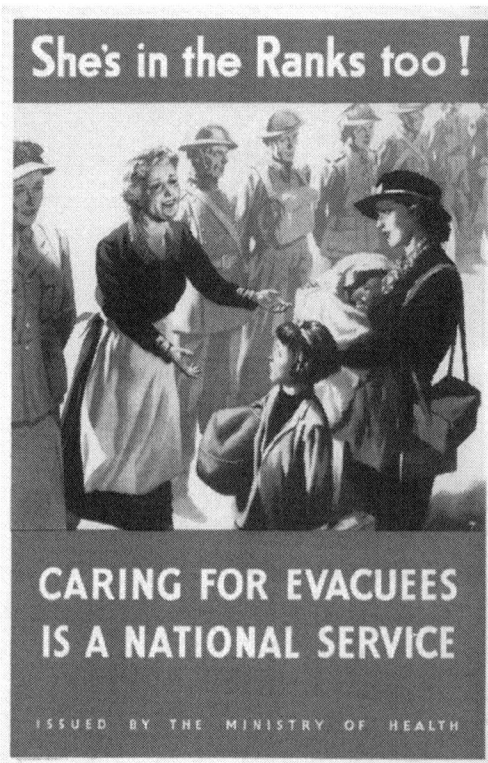

A number of posters and adverts were produced imploring urban families to evacuate their children; asking for families to host evacuees. .

The other significant influx at this time was children. Over the course of the war it is estimated that as many as three and a half million children were evacuated from UK cities, including London, Birmingham and Manchester, where it was anticipated that bombing was a real risk to their lives. Evacuation was not compulsory but, to save their lives, many parents said the most terrible goodbyes to their children and waved them off on their journeys to the countryside. Children from the cities' children's homes were also evacuated to safer places.

North Devon took many of these uprooted, often scared and lonely children, and gave many their first experience of the seaside. In 1944, of the 2,313 children in elementary schools in the Barnstaple Borough, 551 were evacuees. Barnstaple put on facilities in the school holidays to keep the evacuees occupied and entertained with sports and games. The British Restaurant provided dinners.

Once the war was over, some stayed in North Devon and made a life here. Some were able to return to their families and homes, others had lost both. For many, evacuation was a formative experience providing first-hand knowledge of a life different to their own.

Evacuation also had a very significant side effect on a larger scale. The plight of children in cities like Birmingham, London and Manchester had been relatively poorly understood, perhaps not even contemplated. With the arrival of children in rural areas, a far great appreciation developed of what life was like for urban children living in relatively poor areas. And also, what life was like for children living in the many urban children's homes. This greater awareness played a significant part in the creation of the 1948 Children's Act which was to bring an end to children's Cottage Homes.

BARUM WORKHOUSE
1943: Railings

During the War, many iron railings and gates were removed from private and public buildings as part of the war effort. The iron was to be used in the manufacture of ammunition and weapons. Discussing this, the Guardians decided not to give up the railings around the Public Assistance Institution because they were needed to deter residents from absconding.

The last children in the Homes

When the Second World War finally ended in September 1945, the slow process of recovery could begin.

The War had brought to an end the discussion about the future of the children's Cottage Homes in Barnstaple. However, some moves towards modernisation had taken place. An assistant Foster Mother was appointed for each Cottage, rather than there having been one for all three buildings. Uniforms were given to all the staff.

When Frank and Gertrude George retired in 1946. Hubert and Mollie Hicks were appointed as their replacements. They were Superintendent and Matron of the Cottage Homes and had no role in the former workhouse. The tradition of marking the retirement with the gift of an engraved salver to the outgoing Master and Matron was also modernised. Mr and Mrs George were presented with a wireless.

Changes were also afoot in how the role of the Foster Mother was presented to new recruits. While washing and needlework were still essential for the post, there was now a concern to add a focus on family life and the children's well-being. A 1946 job advert for a Foster Mother stated: *"Only persons genuinely interested in providing boys and girls in the County Council Homes with a happy home life on family lines in substitution for their own families need apply, previous experience or training will be an advantage"* and *"the Homes are run on family lines and all staff are expected to mix with the children and be able to plan and enter into their activities and out-of-school occupations"*. Interestingly, the cottage homes at Newton Abbot and Dawlish were recruiting married

---

BARUM WORKHOUSE
A strange fascination

As the average age in the Public Assistance Institution increased, there developed a fascination about it. On a number of occasions the local paper reported on the combined ages of patients who had recently died. In December 1947, they reported that the ages of the six patients who had had died in the past week was 479 years. The oldest patient being 90, the youngest 71.

couples at this point, with single women as assistants, an idea mooted by the Barnstaple Guardians some fifteen years earlier but rejected.

The Christmas celebration of 1948 was held in the Drill Hall on Bear Street rather than in the usual venue of the old workhouse boardroom. Tea was served by William T Buckingham and other members of the Guardians committee and was followed by games and dancing and singing around the piano. The Mayor of Barnstaple, William H Wilkey, dressed as Father Christmas and handed out gifts from the Christmas Tree. The children were also taken to see a pantomime at the John Gay Theatre on Newport Road.

However, within days of this celebration, the decision was taken to close the

---

BARUM WORKHOUSE
Jimmy the Second

In 1943 Jimmy the Donkey received a special mention at the Barnstaple Guardians' Committee meeting. Discussing the Christmas and New Year celebrations which had taken place a few weeks before, all those who had helped to make the event special for the children by sending gifts were thanked. William T Buckingham, the chair, then added "May I say a word on behalf of the donkey? It was a very kind thought to send the carrots, and I think the act deserves our special thanks".

Tragically, in 1947, after twelve years in the Workhouse / PA Institution Jimmy died, reportedly of a broken heart, following the death of the old man in the Institution who had looked after him for so long.

Rosalie Chichester, of Arlington Court, presented the Institution with another donkey who quickly became known as Jimmy the Second.

Homes and place the children in other, more suitable, accommodation.

The was part of a national move to provide better care for children which came about because of the 1946 Curtis Report into the improvements needed for children in care and the Children's Act 1948 which reformed the entire structure of care for children. This landmark legislation formalised an idea that we take for granted now - the idea that children should be treated as individuals. Their needs had be specifically taken into account by local councils who now had the responsibility for providing for them.

For the first time a dedicated Children's Committee with a Children's Officer for Devon was formed in Exeter. The old days of a one size fits all approach to children in care was no longer acceptable. Throughout the country, this sparked a widespread closure of the old children's homes, particularly those which it was thought would cost too much to modernise. The decision was taken to close the Cottage Homes in Barnstaple along with several other children's homes in Devon, and accommodate the children in more modern facilities or foster care. The new children's homes and hostels were to be run on a county-wide basis, separate from adult care, rather than being an add-on to it.

One of the very last trips for the children of the Cottage Homes was a visit to the new model railway at Barnstaple. This was a ride-on 3½ inch gauge train which ran on 250 yards of track in Pottington. Soon after this trip, the children left the Homes for new accommodation marking the very end of the era of the Poor Laws in Barnstaple and the Public Assistance era which followed it.

BARUM WORKHOUSE
1948: The end of the House

In 1948, the National Assistance Act completely abolished all public assistance institutions. While, in 1929, the workhouses had been abolished, the Barnstaple Workhouse had continued in all but name to function very much as the Workhouse had, as a place to accommodate the destitute, the elderly and the infirm. In 1948, this ended and the Public Assistance Institution was closed.

The buildings were reused, after 'an extensive building and redecoration scheme' as the Alexandra Hospital with 169 beds for chronic cases. The former Guardians of the Poor, the Guardians Committee, was also disbanded.

Cottage no. 1 is now in use as the home of Samuels Solicitors

Over the next few decades, the move away from containing (or imprisoning) people who were poor to isolate them from the rest of the community was completed. Instead, children were no longer taken to be put in homes because of being poor or because of the actions of the or parents but it came to be understood that caring for children was based on their own individual needs and working with their family in the context of their situation and their community.

Changes included the professionalisation of people working in residential care with training and qualifications and the introduction of shift work and supervision. The live-in Foster Mother with 24 hour responsibility for a large number of children is now a thing of the past along with the Cottage Homes themselves.

What to do with the Cottage Homes buildings

Across the country, something had to be done about the cottage homes buildings. In the decade after the Second World War ended, hundreds of children were moved out of the old cottage homes into more suitable buildings and the name 'cottage homes' was gone. Most had been built only half a century earlier at great cost to the local ratepayers. There was an understandable desire not to waste this huge investment completely. The Barnstaple Guardians, not completely convinced that the idea of cottage homes was a viable one, had ensured that the Homes were designed to be adaptable for other purposes and, as they now stood on a main road near to the town centre, after they closed, they were a valuable and useful asset without having to be demolished and rebuilt.

In other areas, the cottage homes were demolished. Being large houses in a circle or line in a walled complex, demolishing them to build more modern houses was generally the most cost-effective option. The large tracts of once rural land on which they were originally built, was now often valuable real estate in newly built up areas.

Some cottage homes complexes, however, continued in use as children's homes. Penkhull Cottage Homes in Stoke on Trent along with Kings Norton Union Cottage Homes in Birmingham and others were built as lines of cottage homes along a private road. Finding accommodation for the hundreds of children that lived there would have been a tall order so the decision was taken to change the management structure rather then the physical structure. Thus, each 'cottage' became an individually managed children's home with a reduced number of children living there. The dormitories were split into smaller rooms. The cottage homes schools, infirmaries and chapels were closed as children were now using facilities in the local community instead. The gates were opened and the roads made public. Many of these children's homes were run by a married couple that the children called 'aunt and 'uncle'. If the couple had their own children, they lived there too.

Children who were placed in these children's homes have talked about how, at the time, they didn't see it as odd that they lived in a children's home and there was another children's home next door, and one over the road, and another on the other side. It was only looking back as adults that they could see that an entire street of children's homes was an unusual set up. Ultimately, these children's homes also closed as the focus for looked after children switched more and more to fostering.

In the short space of time that the Barnstaple Cottage Homes existed, a period of just 50 years, many children from around North Devon passed through the cottage doors. Some stayed there for just a few weeks or months, others were there for their entire childhoods. Far larger numbers of children spent time in the workhouse.

The Poor Laws attempted to provide some relief for people in dire straits in this country, whether this was cash payments to help out in a crisis or refuge within the walls of a workhouse or cottage homes. For some the assistance was quite literally life saving. For others, it was a harsh, lonely prison. Some were left vulnerable to exploitation and abuse.

Over time, the reasons for being in need of help have broadened out from absolute poverty into many other family and societal causes. The development of the state benefits system and the NHS, funded through taxation, has enabled millions of people to live independently without the need of residential institutions.

The Poor Laws system, in which a few local ratepayers gave money to the church to hand out to those in need, has grown into a health and social care service costing many billions of pounds. The care team of a workhouse master and Matron and a handful of staff in each town, has grown into a workforce of around 4 million people. There is no full stop in this story however. The way we care for people in need remains in constant flux as we evolve and develop and, hopefully, learn from our past.

Illustrations

Back cover: Artistic impression of cottage homes number 1 in 1902.

All other images are from the author's own collection.

Endnotes

1. The parishes under the Barnstaple Poor Law Union in 1834 were Arlington, Ashford, Atherington, Barnstaple, Berrynarbor, Bishops Tawton, Bittadon, Bratton Fleming, Braunton, Brendon, Challacombe, Combe Martin, Countesbury, East Down, Fremington, Georgeham, Goodleigh, Heanton Punchardon, Highbray, Horwood, Ilfracombe, Instow, Kentisbury, Landkey, Loxhore, Lynton, Martinhoe, Marwood, Mortehoe, Newton Tracy, Parracombe, Pilton, Sherwell, Stoke Rivers, Swimbridge, Tawstock, Trentishoe, West Down, and Westleigh.

2. During this history the spellings of some places have changed including Swymbridge and Morthoe. Combe Martin also changed: at a 1907 meeting of the Guardians "a letter was read from the clerk to the Combmartin Parish Council enclosing a letter from the LGB in which they stated that in the order declaring the constitution of the Barnstaple Union the parish was described as 'Combe Martin'. As it was the ordinary practice to follow that description in official documents issued by the Board. The Parish Council therefore asked that this Board would adopt the above way of spelling Combmartin for the future". I have used the modern spellings throughout.

3. Limbrick, G 2018. Inside the Gates of Children's Cottage Homes. WordWorks, Birmingham

4. According to www.heritagegateway.org.uk, St Mary Magdalene School was on the north-eastern end of what was Lower Maudlin Street (Magdalene was itself pronounced maudlin). Lower Maudlin Street ran parallel to what is now Higher Maudlin Street, on the eastern side. Reform Street was a continuation of Lower Maudlin Street on the south side of Vicarage Street, roughly where Magdalene Lawn is now. Other information about the schools is taken from: Bovett, R. 1989 *Historical Notes on Devon Schools*. Devon County Council

5. The Mental Deficiency Act 1913 attempted to categorise people with learning disabilities or mental illness and paved the way for establishing colonies into which people determined as being mental defective would be sent, potentially for life. The categories of mental deficiency in descending order of perceived seriousness were idiots, imbeciles, and people who were feeble-minded. These terms and the categorisation itself can be seen now as nothing other than inhuman.

By the same author

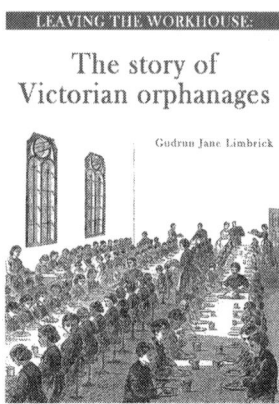

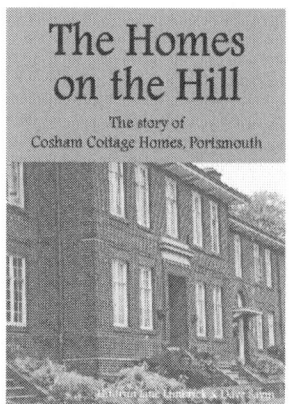

Inside the gates of **children's cottage homes**

LEAVING THE WORKHOUSE:
The story of Victorian orphanages
Gudrun Jane Limbrick

Punishing poverty
The trials of Happy Grace
Gudrun Jane Limbrick

How to research **CHILDHOODS** spent in former **CHILDREN'S HOMES,** orphanages, cottage homes and other children's institutions
Gudrun Jane Limbrick

Deeds of love
The story of Sir Josiah Mason's Orphanage & School, Birmingham
Gudrun Jane Limbrick

THOMAS CORAM'S FOUNDLING HOSPITAL
SAVING LONDON'S ABANDONED BABIES IN THE 18TH CENTURY
GUDRUN LIMBRICK

The children of the Homes
A century of Erdington Cottage Homes

Family Fragments
piecing together a childhood in care
Alan Brain and Gudrun Limbrick

The Homes on the Hill
The story of Cosham Cottage Homes, Portsmouth
Gudrun Jane Limbrick & John Sian

Waterstones